UNIVERSITY

UNIVERSITY

A RECKONING

LEE C. BOLLINGER

 **W. W. NORTON & COMPANY**

Independent Publishers Since 1923

For information about permission to reproduce selections from this book,
write to Permissions, W. W. Norton & Company, Inc.,
500 Fifth Avenue, New York, NY 10110

For information about special discounts for bulk purchases,
please contact W. W. Norton Special Sales at
specialsales@wwnorton.com or 800-233-4830

Manufacturing by Lakeside Book Company
Book design by Patrice Sheridan
Production manager: Julia Druskin

ISBN 978-1-324-12431-3

W. W. Norton & Company, Inc., 500 Fifth Avenue, New York, NY 10110
www.wwnorton.com

W. W. Norton & Company Ltd., 15 Carlisle Street, London W1D 3BS

Authorized EU representative: EAS, Mustamäe tee 50, 10621 Tallinn, Estonia

10 9 8 7 6 5 4 3 2 1

To Jean

CONTENTS

UNIVERSITY

INTRODUCTION

THE UNIVERSITY IS ONE OF THE MOST SUCCESSFUL institutions in American and perhaps human history. I served as a president of both a leading public and a leading private university for just over a quarter century. I know universities intimately, and, while I have my fair share of criticisms about them, the fact is they are amazing places. It is commonly pointed out, with complete justification, that almost everything good in our modern existence can be traced back in some way to work done in our academic institutions. This is well worth repeating over and over again. But this is not the only test of success. I challenge anyone to spend a day, a week, or more in any university—sitting in on classes, attending lectures, meeting with students, visiting a laboratory, being part of a seminar—and not come away deeply impressed, indeed invigorated, about the human potential to know and to grasp something of our existence. You realize how remarkably serious these places are; you see how the expertise and knowledge possessed and exhibited by professors and students is accompanied by a special intellectual character and spirit of independence. It is no surprise that people from all over the nation and the world, often at great sacrifice, wish to attend these institutions and take the benefits offered. Even the fiercest critics will turn around and do everything they can to assist their child in being admitted to the institution they are criticizing. I know.

The American university is the standard for the world in higher education. It attracts some portion of the most talented individuals of each generation to spend their lives as professors trying to preserve and expand the accomplishments of the human mind and to introduce the youth of each new generation into the mysteries of existence.

And yet, this moment has brought severe and unprecedented challenges to the continued existence and viability of the university and the broader system of universities in this country. The most immediate threats come from our own federal government.

The Trump administration has put the nation on a trajectory of disregarding fundamental principles and norms, indeed constitutional rights, and this dangerous course has focused, in part, on universities. In March 2025, the administration started with Columbia University, my home, by threatening the withdrawal of federal funds intended for science and biomedical research. The purported basis for this attack was that the university had failed to protect Jewish students against antisemitism in the period of the protests following the massacre in Israel by Hamas on October 7, 2023. That failure, the government claimed, was prohibited by Title VI of the Civil Rights Act, which conditions receiving federal funds on complying with the antidiscrimination rules. Other universities have faced similar challenges from the administration, Harvard in particular. Still other universities have faced the Damoclean sword of funding suspensions for operating programs that promote diversity, equity, and inclusion (DEI), and one, the University of Pennsylvania, had been confronted with the same punishment for permitting a transgender athlete to participate in a woman's sport, even though the university was following the law and regulations in place at the time. The "remedies" the government is seeking go infinitely beyond anything ever demanded before over concerns about violating Title VI. These include putting academic departments in so-called receivership, developing plans for more ideologically diverse faculty, changing disciplinary procedures for student misconduct, transforming academic governance, and monitoring admissions processes.[1]

Because federal funds constitute such a significant proportion of every university's annual budget, universities have rightly claimed that they are facing an existential threat, one that could only be alleviated by essentially allowing the federal government to run their institutions and curtail academic freedom. Columbia chose the path of conciliation and negotiation with the Trump administration, which led to a settlement. Harvard chose resistance and negotiation, receiving an injunction from the lower court that blocked the government's demands and the suspension of funds. Harvard claims that these demands violated both the statute (Title VI) and the First

Amendment by intruding into traditional academic decision-making. Some sixty or more other universities are in the government crosshairs awaiting their fates.[2]

The Trump administration has taken additional actions that threaten the viability of the modern university, including restricting foreign student visas and challenging existing accreditation processes and standards.[3]

The federal government is not alone in launching an assault on academic institutions. Several states have also tried to seize control of the inner workings of public universities, forbidding professors from teaching certain ideas or demanding that they emphasize others favored by government officials.[4]

Nor is this kind of extraordinary attack confined to universities. Similar threats have been leveled at major law firms that have represented people and parties that the administration identifies as their political opponents. Furthermore, press and major media outlets have faced a variety of largely baseless lawsuits, accusations, and investigations involving claims of defamation, criminal activity, and other actions deemed unacceptable by the administration.[5]

We are, in short, witnessing a tectonic shift in America toward the use of authoritarian tactics that threaten our democratic form of government. Long-established norms, hard won over decades and centuries, are being cast aside. The university is among the first (along with the press) of the major independent institutions in society to feel the brunt of this new and frightening transformation. These institutions have struggled with how to respond and, in many important respects, have failed to forestall the attacks.

But these are not the only challenges to universities in the modern era. There are some, for example, who believe that the new technologies of communication will make the traditional model of university research and education outmoded. They see universities as inefficient in the methods of doing research and especially in educating students. Just as the traditional press in America found out too late that people would not always go to their front porch to pick up the daily newspaper and read it over breakfast and coffee but instead would find the "news" on their mobile phones at any time of day or night and from any source they chose, so something analogous will eventually happen with university education. We have watched as the basic business model of the traditional press has been demolished by the openness of the internet, when literally everyone can become a "publisher," so it will happen to universities, the thinking goes, when everyone can also become a "teacher." This challenge raises a question: What would be lost in this new world of open education through the internet? And now artificial intelligence is posing profound questions about how we teach, research, learn, and acquire knowledge and skills.[6]

This is a moment of grave significance if you care about universities and believe, as I do, that they are one of the wonders of the modern world. When you are under attack, however, one clear benefit is that you are forced to dig deeper and be clearer in your own mind about what you believe and why you believe it to be true. You can see vividly that the fortifications and barriers erected in the past to protect our values are now clearly insufficient. The premise of this book is that we need to consider, not just react to, the current attacks and plan for a better future, a more secure nation and world. We can see how unprepared we have been at every level, from the university to the U.S. Constitution itself.

This book is an attempt at a reckoning—an attempt to confront the crisis and reimagine who we are now and for the future. To do that we need to look at two major American institutions, not just the university but also the First Amendment. The fact is that, while universities over the last century were becoming the research and educational powerhouses that they are today, so the First Amendment was becoming the backbone of the nation's commitment to knowledge and the search for truth in the public realm. It is now in the convergence of these once-parallel developments that we can find the best path forward.

The story of the First Amendment is remarkable, and it is entwined with that of the university. The U.S. Supreme Court first began interpreting the First Amendment only in 1919, even though it had been part of the Constitution since the Bill of Rights was added in 1791. But over the past century the courts have issued thousands of decisions that altogether create a jurisprudence of freedom of speech unmatched by any nation before or since. For universities there has been a parallel development. As the jurisprudence of the First Amendment was beginning, so was the transition of universities from a small base of institutions engaged in teaching elites to becoming what they are today: world-class, world-defining research powerhouses that have also advanced knowledge in profound ways and educated millions of students from here and around the world. In sum, over the past one hundred years, we have witnessed the spectacular rise of two areas of American life that define our nation.[7]

These two institutions—the constitutional principles of freedom of speech and press and the network of universities— are deeply interconnected, interrelated, and mutually reinforcing. They share the same ends and propose the same way of life. Both follow the same path and do so with unique and even extreme forms. Together they set the national course for the pursuit of knowledge as well as some other fundamental values we hold dear in America, such as the rule of law, the separation of branches of government, and the key role of the press. They are essential elements of a democracy in which citizens are free to pursue the most important ends of life, including understanding our existence and the natural world.

At this point in their development, the First Amendment and the university are extremely complex in their structures and operations. In so many respects, they have been designed in highly unusual, indeed in counterintuitive, ways and taken forms that it is doubtful anyone would create from scratch. Under the First Amendment, we now are committed to an extreme openness to ideas, with even the most noxious opinions protected against government censorship. In the university world, there are many restrictions on what can be expressed in scholarship and teaching, but there also remains an abnormal openness to ideas. Their shared dedication to the discovery of truth is what binds them in a common enterprise, as does their keen awareness of the need to beware of our natural impulses that run counter to the quest for knowledge.

This book will show how the university and the First Amendment fortify each other and how the latter can provide the protection that the university today so clearly needs. In the face of the attacks from the current president, we need nothing less than a new conception of the role of the university in a free society under the First Amendment. The traditional arguments for why we should value universities—that they advance civilization, that they are an engine of economic and social growth, that they are a competitive advantage for the nation in the world, and that they educate our youth and prepare our citizens and attempt to equalize the opportunities available to them—are valid. But these arguments do not begin to capture and articulate the deeper and foundational role of the university in the American constitutional system. If the press is the unofficial fourth branch of the system, the university is the fifth—and even more so now as the press is in decline.

The book has three chapters. In the first, I explore the structure of the university and why that structure has contributed to its great success. I think most people in the United States, even many of us inside the university, do not fully understand how universities operate and, most important, why they have been successful. We all need to understand this in order to appreciate their fundamental role in the society, their contributions to the common good, their vulnerabilities, and their potential to do so much more.

In the second chapter, I explore the First Amendment, tracing its history from its true beginning in 1919 to the present and explaining what it has become. It is, to be sure, a raucous regime we have created, a point that will turn out to be important in understanding how the university finds its niche in the layers of American life. To understand the First Amendment is also to understand universities and their role. To study the First Amendment is to discover both the limits on government power over universities and also how the profound values expressed in our foundational documents become embodied in our lives, so to speak. My highest hope would be to see our constitutional jurisprudence develop a robust principle of freedom of the university. But even if that does not come to fruition, it is still critical for us to understand that the value and role of the university emanate from the bedrock of American society. Not all constitutional principles are those the Supreme Court declares it is ready to enforce.

In the third and final chapter, I try to envision an expanded role for the university, one that will offer it shelter from government meddling in its essential truth-seeking mission. Then we can begin to imagine what needs to be done now and in the future to secure, and derive the full benefits from, this right.

This is a deeply personal book, and not only because of the nature and trajectory of my career. I have thought about everything I explore in these pages for more or less all of my life. Like many of my generation, I found my way to the university from a middle-class family, attending public schools in rural areas of western America. My father was the editor and publisher of a small-town daily newspaper. From him and that experience, including working at the paper, I came to understand journalism and the public role of the press, imbued with a very strong sense of public service and autonomy. From being a young law professor, I felt the excitement and self-doubts that came with the ambition to master a subject and to make a notable contribution to its advancement. From the time I was a dean of a law school, I learned how a scholar becomes part of a larger field of inquiry and a part of the university. And, then, as a university president I learned how the entire system of universities operates. Throughout everything I felt an identification of purpose that infuses everything I say here.

Much of what I write in this book will be labeled idealistic. I am not ashamed of that. There is much to be critical of and doubtful about when talking about the First Amendment or universities, and I have offered my critiques and doubts over time. But there are times in life when you are facing the loss of something you treasure or cherish and all the criticisms and critiques become secondary—when you feel it is necessary to stop short and say, *Hold on*. Instead of being narrow-minded and dangerously fixated on problems, we need to work to preserve and build on a way of life that, for all its faults, for all those who are dissatisfied with their place in it, is nevertheless precious. This book offers a positive case for the continuation of the university.

At the root of this project is the simple idea expressed beautifully more than four centuries ago by the French essayist Michel de Montaigne: "There is no desire more natural than the desire for knowledge. We try all the ways that can lead us to it. When reason fails us, we use experience." To be sure, there are many ultimate values in life, among them love and friendship. But the desire for knowledge is among the first, and the First Amendment and universities embrace it as their mission. A life with *only* the desire to know would be arid; but a life without it would be meaningless.[8]

CHAPTER ONE

THE UNIVERSITY

WHAT IS THE FUNDAMENTAL PURPOSE OF THE UNIVER-
sity? It is deceptively simple to state: Universities are intended
to preserve and advance human knowledge about the human
condition, about life and about the natural world, and to pass
human knowledge and the capacities to pursue it on to succeeding generations. Now, the answer becomes instantly more
complex when you start asking questions about what is this
"knowledge" that we seek to preserve and add to. What we
take to be worthy of "knowing" is always a contested matter.
Identifying from all the things that are known what we want to
preserve can be a fraught inquiry. We are always making judgments about what knowledge to embrace and what to discard
or jettison. Furthermore, we must appreciate that "preserving
and advancing knowledge" is a fluid process that is more accu-
rately described as an ongoing conversation among many people, not some fixed idea stated on a blackboard and memorized
by everyone. A library contains knowledge, but a continuous

discussion is an even more vital and important form of knowledge than the opportunity alone to check out a book.

But how does a university "advance knowledge"? Through its unique structure. By any standards, and certainly by the standards of organizational theory, universities are strange creatures, even bizarre and counterintuitive in how they operate. And yet they work. Why is that so? Let's start with the professor.

THE PROFESSOR

There is a common stereotype of the senior professor—as someone who is an expert in some arcane area of knowledge, perhaps smart in certain ways but a simpleton in normal life, who (as the saying goes) knows more and more about less and less, and who teaches only maybe five or six hours a week and usually with the aid of faded teaching notes, with an air of boredom at repeating the same things to yet another group of seemingly younger and younger students who in all probability have concerns on their minds very different from the content of the course. With the practice of tenure, the professor lives without constraints. No one runs the university; the professor runs amok.

This is far from the truth. Every year I was president, I taught my First Amendment course to undergraduates, in part because I loved their openness and in part to symbolize that the university valued the youngest among us. When doing so, I would always spend hours preparing my mind and attention to the subject of the day's class, no matter how many times I had taught it before. It is always a performance to be in front of a class, not unlike an actor in theater, and each class is unique. The one constant is the level of intellect in the room, and the professor must attend to it or pay the consequences of critical evaluations, where students are merciless in saying what they thought of the course and the teacher. The proof is always in just how exhausted a teacher is after the class is finished. You need a good hour or two to recuperate, but few things in life are more exhilarating than teaching a good class. I know this not just from my own experience in the classroom but from knowing hundreds if not thousands of professors over the years.

We begin with the professor because it is with this figure that the primary academic power resides within any university. This is mainly a function of tenure, which is more or less a guarantee of lifetime employment for individual faculty, but it is not exclusively related to that. What is expected of the professor, and what is afforded the professor in return?

First, to be a professor is indeed to be an expert, a specialist, in an academic subject. You are expected to know literally all that has been thought and said about the field—an unrealizable goal. The "field" is something created by your peers and the university system as a whole, but it can be shaped by the faculty member over time. I may be an expert in the "First Amendment," but even within that field there may be topics I emphasize much more than others (perhaps I am more of an expert on media and the First Amendment or the internet and free speech). Over time I may take up new fields, but they will almost always be nearby to the ones I began with. One should not underestimate how enlivening it can be to accept the challenge of mastering a field of knowledge. This is the worthy mission of a lifetime. Almost always these are subjects humans have wondered and thought about for centuries, and you are able to tap into the richness of the thoughts these efforts have yielded.

The second thing expected of a professor is that he or she says something original and important about the field. One cannot overstate just how important this expectation is or how difficult it is. I remember well when I began as a law professor the feeling of having nothing new to add to what had already been said. It seemed preposterous. When I confessed this to a senior professor, he responded that he had a file in his desk full of ideas he would probably never get to. I thought if only I could have one . . .

So, it is hard to master a body of knowledge and then say something new and important when others, almost certainly smarter than you, have pored over the subject for years. And, yet, as hard as it is to do, this expectation is the core of what makes universities distinctive and what makes them the ideal settings for advancing knowledge. To many, it is naïve, even silly, to expect everyone to say something novel and important, since it is rare that important new advancements are made. But it is precisely in the level of difficulty that the brilliance of the expectation resides. When everyone feels the pressure, the likelihood of significant advancements is increased. And, as Samuel Johnson remarked, "self-confidence is the first requisite to great undertakings." In any event, this is the key premise. It is also notable that this is also an expectation even of students. The impossible expectation placed on its denizens gives a dynamism to the American university that is unmatched.[1]

Every professor, every field, draws inspiration from the great minds who have previously upset conventional ways of seeing the world. They did not flinch in the face of an opportunity to launch and further an intellectual revolution. Their ideas may have been unpopular, but that did not deter them from proceeding. This is because the purpose is to see what has not been seen before, to grasp some new flicker of light that might lead to a revelation that will change our world. Every field has its spectacular shifts in perspective, which may have taken decades or even centuries to become generally accepted, but they mark a watershed in human understanding and give way to still other new opportunities to grasp the unknown.

Every single professor is keenly aware of these moments of transformational discovery, and those stand as the benchmark for their own work. Of course, most, or nearly all, faculty find their own level of investigation. Not every professor needs to, or should, try to fundamentally change their field. One of the early lessons you take in as you begin your scholarly career is how important it is to find the right questions for you to ask.

There are natural and persistent tensions. The scholarly world is always seeking to find some equilibrium between pursuing knowledge for the sake of knowledge and being in alignment with the current interests and needs of the world. To what extent should science be focused on finding cures for diseases, or solving problems of the environment, or creating life-changing products? Or to what extent should scientists pursue the knowledge that seems important without regard to its ultimate human benefits? The same questions arise in the social sciences and professional schools such as law.

Compare the roles of journalism and academic scholarship. In many instances, there is an overlap between the subjects of the "news" and of scholarly inquiry. Journalism must inform us of what it can know now. The scholar can take longer and go deeper. It is a good division of labor when journalists meet the need to know as much as we can now, and scholars stand ready to seek all we can know with a longer time frame.

This, too, reveals an important truth about the university, namely that much of what is done within it is connected to the public sphere. The university is not "political," in the sense of having a partisan motivation, but it does speak to what are often public issues, or should be public issues, from the standpoint of the scholarly process. There is a kind of idealism that pervades academic work. It has many sources, but it is a pronounced disposition (along with many others, such as being innately skeptical, wary of easy answers, and always ready to look beneath the surface of things for potential unseen truths). It is part of a long American tradition of establishing foundational values against which we are continually comparing ourselves. The most noteworthy instance of this has been with the project of eliminating invidious discrimination against Black Americans and overcoming the centuries of mistreatment they have endured. This has set in motion a broader effort to expand the groups identified as suffering from unfair treatment. At various points, including in the current moment, there has been a backlash against these efforts, but that does not nullify the efforts to make America a more-just society. And so many of these efforts have originated in, and also shaped, the scholarship taking place in the American university.

Scholarly work does not make the compromises necessary to keep profits high or adjustments to one's values to accommodate contrary political interests. Furthermore, it is in the nature of scholarship, just as it is in journalism, to hold the government and the society to account. I always keep in mind the comment of a major American journalist who said (in a private moment) that he wakes up every morning and asks himself, "I wonder what the bastards are up to today." When your job entails looking critically at what is happening and holding a mirror up to the world, it is to be expected—and in a mature society desired—to have institutions such as the press and the university ready to be, and fearless in being, critical.

When taking stock of what university scholarship yields, one must look at the whole. I personally know that the work of many faculty, even in the most prestigious institutions, is not "transformational." I do not mean to say the work is not an important contribution or does not add novel insights on important questions. I just cannot say that the world has been significantly changed by the work. What I can say, however, is that across the university world there has been work of dazzling creativity and significance. And I can further say that this work would not have happened but for the context in which it arose.

The myth of the solitary genius still prevails in the twenty-first century. Yet many accomplished people will admit that their achievements emerged out of a context and a culture that shaped and supported and nurtured their ideas until their ideas became something remarkable. We know, through experience, that very often we do not even understand our own ideas until we hear other people repeat them to us. I also do not believe that it would have been possible at some theoretical starting point, if every would-be scholar was sitting in a long row, to select those who would eventually make such seminal discoveries.

The university is a magnificent institution not because it is great in every facet, but because viewed as a whole it is spectacular and without any peer.

The third thing expected of a professor is that their scholarship must be made fully available to the public. This is not a trivial matter and speaks to the public service role that universities assume. When one thinks about international faculty and students participating in research at the American university, this fact becomes especially vivid. The philosophy has always been that knowledge is a public good, and we will share it with the best and brightest from all over the planet, who will then perhaps return to their countries and expand the world's capacity to know. There is no concept of keeping knowledge at home.

A fourth condition of being a professor is that you also teach. Everyone must teach students. Universities are not divided into research faculty and teaching faculty. You take on the responsibility of bringing the next generation into your field, a generation capable of being even more successful than yours. Universities are not just research institutes, nor are they just research institutes with a little teaching on the side. Being with students, with youth, is a principal assignment and one most faculty (not all) take very seriously. Nor is it an easy task. All the time I was a dean or president, I would speak with alumni who would say something like "I think I would like to take up teaching. I've had so much experience in life, and now I'd like to share that with young people." Little do they realize that that is not what teaching in a university really is, nor is teaching that simple. To be sure, it's a worthy sentiment, but it is almost always completely wrong about what we really do. Students are incredibly intelligent and astute, and one of the last things they want out of a course is a collection of one's anecdotes about any field of life. What is taught in a university course is something far different, more substantive and in-depth. It is many things, but it is mostly an immersion into a realm of thought by people who have studied a subject and attempted to master it. In every field, students are brought into a body of deep knowledge, with contested ideas and broad insights that carry over into life broadly.

The fifth characteristic of being a professor is perhaps the hardest to talk about but also the most important. It is the very distinctive state of mind, or intellectual character, that everyone is expected to bring to the research and teaching that happens on a campus. It is a disposition that defines what it is to be in the academy. I call it the *scholarly temperament*. It entails many norms and practices—and punishments for violations—

that everyone must acquire and live by in order to be a full member of a university. To me, the strength of the intellectual norms of the scholarly temperament were revealed when I became a president. The university presidency is mostly an academic position in nature, but you play other roles, too: the businessperson, the press person, and the politician. I recall the sense of astonishment that I could set aside the strictures of the scholarly temperament and think and answer with greater freedom. You can answer a question with what you choose to say, avoid the need to give reasons for your answer, and deflect a conversation into areas you prefer to speak about. None of these moves would have worked very well in a faculty presentation, but they worked perfectly well in a political context. The experience was a stark contrast to that of being a scholar or teacher where the demands and constraints on your thinking are very powerful and deeply instilled.

In mastering your field or advocating for your ideas about the field, you cannot just declare that you believe what you are saying is true and leave it at that. On the contrary, you must *demonstrate* that you have grasped all that has come before you, and you must explain in detail how what you are proposing fits into that body of thought. You must give reasons why your ideas are different and important for others to hear and think through. If anyone else has contributed to your thinking, you must openly and fully acknowledge and credit that contribution. Most important, you must confront opposing perspectives and show genuine recognition of their merit when it is due. You must entertain—really entertain—the possibility that you are wrong. And, finally, you must be willing to change your mind if the evidence calls for it.

The scholarly community, whether in the research setting or the classroom, is made up of minds that strive to hold simultaneously every possible way of looking at a problem while recommending that each single member of the community have one that is preferred above the others. A professor is not a lawyer in the courtroom, or a politician in a public debate, or a religious leader—all of whom must demonstrate unconditional belief in a position they are expected to defend. Rather in a university you must be considered, thoughtful, open to alternatives, and welcoming of arguments that might lead you to have a change of mind. A good academic takes pride in knowing that to be proved wrong is not necessarily a failure but, at least when well-defended and interesting, potentially a contribution to the ongoing search for better ideas.

Many years ago, a very distinguished colleague who was the world's expert in a large and complex field was confronted by a student who disputed the characterization of a particular provision in a statute that the professor had offered. It didn't read the way the professor said, the student asserted. When the professor looked, he realized the student was right and, for all these years, he had been misreading the section. I asked him what his reaction was, to which he responded that he laughed in delight at his error and the student correcting him. That seemed to me then, and now, to reflect the true spirit of the professorial character. So much we think we know is not fully accurate, and bearing that in mind always is the intellectual ambition we should hold out for ourselves.

The scholarly temperament is not easy to hold on to. It cuts against our natural impulses, which are to have beliefs and to defend these beliefs against attack. I have seen this countless times in the university. The debates within fields can become fights, and vicious ones at that. There are professors who act in bad faith or who cling to clearly obsolete ideas simply because these ideas are theirs. More prosaically, in anything as large as a university, or better yet, the national (and international) system of universities, there will be many variations in intellectual attitude. Sometimes there will be outliers who fit more closely in the "advocate" role—individuals who seem committed to particular perspectives and are dismissive of alternative visions. I myself have advocated at times for hiring an individual who had such characteristics, for the reason that the individual's work was outstanding in the new insights put forward.

Everyone always says that we should "be open-minded," but rarely does anyone explain why that is so hard to do or how to get the correct balance of open-mindedness and belief. That difficulty—and the distance between ideal and practice—is a central theme of this book, and we will encounter it again and again but especially in the next chapter, on the origins of the First Amendment and the premises on which the edifice has been constructed.

To be sure, the scholarly temperament is not the only way to arrive at truth or knowledge. In a courtroom, the normal process of finding the truth is to have two advocates, each of whom does everything possible to articulate their position, and then a judge or jury that mediates between these opposing positions. What might be called the *judicial temperament* is similar to the scholarly temperament, but not identical. The key point is that, in the world of the university, the intellectual process is completely distinctive.

All of this suggests another significant feature of the university world. The special and narrow focus, and the constraints placed on the mind at work, can happen at scale only if everyone—faculty and students—is part of a separate and discrete community and in almost all cases in close physical contact. Contrary those who advocate moving higher education to an online system, the physical existence of a university, the campus, is a little world unto itself. This physical world creates and reinforces a "culture" that enhances the seriousness of and commitment to the general mission and the norms of behavior that make that mission possible. Something that is hard to do becomes easier when everyone around you is doing it, too.

The final aspect of being a professor is, in many ways, the most unique element in academic life: the system of tenure. This is where the organizational structure becomes most unusual, to many people even bizarre. To give an "employee" of an organization the promise of a lifetime position seems to be a recipe for inefficiency and laziness. Why would anyone with a totally secure job work hard when there would be virtually no or few negative consequences for poor performance? But it does not fail in that expected way. The system of tenure enhances the appeal to the most talented people to join the academic mission and stimulates professors to perform better.

Imagine that you have completed your undergraduate studies or your professional school studies (for example, law, business, medicine). You are among the very top students in your class, with a fine, or perhaps outstanding, record as a student. You are at the point of considering whether to try to become a professor or to pursue other options and careers. What factors would you weigh in your mind?

Given how well you have performed, you most certainly will have many possible routes to consider. Virtually all of them other than joining the academic world will provide a promise of much greater income over your lifetime. But most of those will offer far less control over your life, at least until you establish yourself many years down the road. You are also less likely to have much or any job security. You may also feel you have a calling to the academic life—many do.

If you decide to go the route of becoming a professor, it will not be easy. It will look something like this: For those other than the students graduating from the professional schools, you will need to spend a number of years, usually five or more, in graduate school pursuing an expertise in a given field and writing your dissertation. Now, whether armed with a PhD or a professional school degree, you are ready to join the market for a job as a professor. If you are successful at landing a position—no small thing, these days, with few jobs open in many fields—you will now have to teach students and pursue a research program. You will become more and more specialized in your field of expertise, and you will have to show that you are contributing to the knowledge of your area of focus. After a period of about five to seven years, you are "up for tenure." A general and in-depth assessment of your teaching and your scholarly work by experts in your field will lead to a judgment about whether you have the promise of major work over the course of your career. It is a projection from what you have done about what you might accomplish in the decades ahead.

If the decision is unfavorable, you may well have reached the end of your academic career, unless you are at a top institution, in which case you might have a chance at landing a tenure-track job at a less prestigious college or university. If the decision is favorable, you now have a lifetime to accomplish what you hope to achieve. Now the real expectations will set in. It is not uncommon for recently tenured faculty to feel depressed (not in a clinical sense!), for now their lifetime dream is realized but the performance will be very difficult. There will be a few more promotions along the way (from associate professor to full professor, an appointment to a named chair, and so on), but none has anything close to the consequence of the initial decision of being granted tenure. Your salary will increase but only incrementally on an annual basis, with some bumps at certain milestones in your career. In all likelihood, rarely will a raise be more than 10 or 20 percent, and rarely will your salary come close to what you could have made in other endeavors. You have traded income for job security and the freedom to pursue an area of knowledge that intrigues you. You have also decided to face the challenge to be one of the original minds exploring that area of inquiry, all the while being part of a larger community of people doing more or less the same in their areas of expertise and specialization. I once heard someone say of a professor that he or she has no concept of having "a boss." That comment has a kernel of truth, but, as we shall see, is not entirely accurate.

Here, then, is the arrangement made with each professor. You, the university, will give me tenure for life, and I will give you my life for tenure. I will be passionate in devoting myself to exploring the body of knowledge in my field and to bringing youth into my universe. I will be a worthy member of the university and a full fellow of the community of peers at other universities. I will be a good colleague in my institution. I will to the best of my ability adhere to, preserve, protect, and defend the scholarly temperament. And I, together with my colleagues, will defend the autonomy of the university against encroachments from within and without.

THE SCHOOL

From the professor, we move up the institutional ladder to the department or division or school. This is the next layer of the university. Here you have the entire group of faculty who are all experts in some facet of a more general field. You have all the faculty who focus on history, or political science, or biology, or law. Everyone is tenured or tenure track, along with others who hold positions of clinical faculty or research faculty and so on. What binds the group together is that each member shares an academic focus on the broader area, be it chemistry or physiology or computer science. This will be an important part of your intellectual and social life. Gatherings in the faculty commons, workshops over drafts, formal lectures to attend, and shared social events—these will shape who you are and provide a professional context in which your performance as a scholar and teacher will be judged.

At this level of the university, the faculty make important decisions over such issues as whom to hire or promote; what the curriculum for the students should be and for what degrees; which students should be admitted and what grading standards should be. There will be a dean or department chair, who inevitably will be chosen from within the field. What remains true here is that the responsibility for the research agenda and the manner of teaching one's courses rests almost entirely with the individual professor. The school or department is the "home" of each professor, and important collective decisions are taken there as a group, but the norm is to leave individual faculty members in nearly full control over their intellectual work. The dean or chair knows to respect that autonomy.

This is also the point at which one begins to see alumni involvement. Almost every school or college within the university will have something called board of visitors, or even occasionally "Overseers." These entities are explicitly meant to be strictly advisory to the school and to the university administration. But the way they actually act is often quite different, and more influential.

THE PRESIDENT AND THE
CENTRAL ADMINISTRATION

From here one moves up the ladder of institutional authority to the president. There is a direct line from the schools to the central administration, which is presided over by the president. The president appoints a provost, who is the chief academic officer, as well as several other executive vice presidents overseeing areas of finances, alumni relations and philanthropy, public relations, legal matters, and so on. The president and the provost oversee the entire institution. But fundamental academic decisions—what to teach, what to research, and so on—are made and executed at the grassroots level, and that reality is respected by the central administration. Academic decisions over matters such as promotion and tenure do reach this top level, but the review and final decision rely heavily on the evaluation set at the individual school.

There is a major philosophical question here. For many, especially among the faculty, the central administration is expected to have little, perhaps even no, involvement in the "academic" decisions of the institution. Yes, the university must be managed, and there are appointments to be made, such as the deans of schools. The president must also represent the university in a variety of settings, preside over the countless ceremonies and events that make up the academic calendar, and raise money. But, essentially, the primary role of the central administration is to support what is properly called the "infrastructure" of the university in which the faculty and departments and schools determine the research and educational functions.

Many presidents fall easily into this mode. There is always much to do—committees and task forces to form and manage, search committees to chair, an endless number of serious issues that must be resolved, budgetary questions to examine and decide—and, if you let them take over your workday, they will. Early on in my career as a president, I realized that there is a bargain to be struck with the deans. Even though you have appointed them and annually determine their compensation, the truth is that deans very quickly realize that their fates are determined by their faculty. They accept general oversight as necessary, but questions about the directions or quality of their academic mission are regarded as solely within their purview. They appreciate additional resources and other benefits, but only insofar as those fit within the idea of the autonomy of their school. The bargain is this: From the dean's perspective, he or she will praise the president for doing a great job if in return the president does not meddle in the school's business. This represents a general phenomenon in the governance of universities, namely that the true power or authority over the core functions resides at the base of the institution, with the faculty first and foremost and with the school secondarily. And this creates what I have long referred to as the powerful centrifugal forces that characterize a university.

I personally rejected this view, at least in part: I always thought that the proper role of the president and the central administration is to resist these forces—not completely, but to a degree that is healthy for the overall work of the institution. Yet the lesson at this level, too, is that the university is dedicated to the pursuit of knowledge, and the experts themselves are largely running the show. This makes it imperative that much of the leadership come from within the academic side of the university, which, in fact, is typically the case.

This does not mean, of course, that the president and the provost alone decide what intellectual interventions are important to undertake. There are many ways to draw deans and faculty into these kinds of issues and decisions. But the intellectual role of the president is important.

There are all kinds of ways in which research and teaching can go awry and not be dealt with effectively by faculty alone. New fields emerge that may be resisted or inadequately addressed by faculty. That may mean sponsoring new initiatives or even establishing new schools. At Columbia, we did that by creating the first Climate School in the nation to focus more work and attention on the issues surrounding climate change. Often there will be a need to bring faculty from across the institution together to do work on subjects that are not primarily covered by a single discipline or field. And, occasionally, a department or school may have become so fractured and incapable of exercising academic control that it must be put under university control (a process referred to in the academic world as "receivership").[2]

The main point here is that the level of university administration also contributes to an important substantive engagement with the fundamental work of research and teaching.

THE BOARDS AND THE ALUMNI

Finally, there are the boards of regents or trustees. These vary in how they are selected, their scale, and their involvement. In public universities, boards are either appointed by the governor of the state or elected (as was true at the University of Michigan). In private universities, board members are typically self-perpetuating, and members may be chosen from alumni or people outside the university community. Boards are burdened with an ultimate fiduciary responsibility for the institution. That includes at a minimum making sure that the finances are in good order, that the law and regulations are complied with, that the procedures and rules of the institution are followed, and so on. But there is a distinct difference between a board of a private corporation and a board of a university in the degree to which they become involved in the management of the organization. A university board gives much more deference to the academic mission than the board of a private corporation gives to the personal preferences of management. Since virtually none of the members of the typical university board will be from the academy, and since the culture of the intellectual life within the institution is highly distinctive, deference is expected and generally afforded. To take one example, review of promotion and tenure decisions is perfunctory by boards. The same is true with respect to which intellectual fields to pursue, which students to admit, or which curriculum to set, and so on.

There have been significant changes in the role of corporate and nonprofit boards in my lifetime. Once the role was simply to be supportive and helpful, such as by making or securing donations. But the idea of actually overseeing and running things had not yet emerged. And there was a good reason: Directors, trustees, and others, who spend little time in the role, cannot possibly understand things to the degree needed to be a responsible operator, and find it best to leave the hard tasks to others who have all the knowledge and skills. But in the era of corporate reform in the latter part of the twentieth century, one place reform-minded people looked was to boards, and with a theory in hand that board members should be made legally responsible for ensuring good organizational behavior and would provide a good check on misbehavior especially among management, reformers pushed this to become more and more the norm.[3]

This change has then been brought increasingly to universities. We should not be surprised by this, given that virtually all of these trustees are outsiders and often come from the corporate world, where they have become accustomed to the active board model. In general, I don't think this has been a problem, but when it is, it's a serious one. The boards of corporations usually are made up of people from the corporate world, and they therefore know that universe. It's quite the opposite with boards of universities. The lack of familiarity with what universities are really about can, at times, be striking. And when trustees believe themselves "responsible" for the institution in a final sense, it can lead to very damaging and out-of-control board behavior.

I have been told by board members more times than I can count that "the key role of the board is to hire and fire the president." This is usually said as an acknowledgment that the board does not interfere in the academic decision-making of the institution, and selecting the president is the only way in which the board exerts influence into that process. One might hear similar statements in corporate boardrooms as well. For universities, however, it is a serious misstatement of reality and of what is academically desirable. In the university, it is everyone—faculty first and foremost, but also students and alumni—who think they, too, should hire and fire the president. For the leader of a university should embody and represent the whole, at all times. If you ever feel you are in a state of opposition to your faculty, it is time to consider returning to the faculty.

As for alumni, every university seeks to engage its graduates (and those with intimate connections to the university, such as parents of students). There is a strong sense of community among faculty and current and former students that characterizes the modern American university. The motives for this are many, but in its purest form it is a feeling that together we have shared something profound in life: the process of learning together, the formation of a bond around the aim of being serious about knowing things that count and matter, out of which experience there is a lifelong connection. There are also feelings of identification that are natural in a world in which institutions compete with one another, in everything from prestige and reputation to victories on the athletic fields and other contests. And on the university side, there are hopes and expectations of contributions, mostly in the form of monetary gifts that will support the activities of faculty research and the education of students.

One of the ways in which alumni become involved in the governance of the university is through boards of advisors established for individual schools (and sometimes departments) within a given university. These boards are not formally intended to be part of the official governance of the institution but rather are advisory in nature. They play a more or less active role as determined by the individual deans. At times, however, they can become more than thoughtful advisors and instead turn into quasi decision-makers, sometimes even at the invitation of the deans. This should not happen, but it is a risk and must be managed, just as boards of trustees and regents need to be appropriately restrained. We will return to this question later.

The upshot is that within universities, the intent is to insulate the faculty from control or interference, with some qualifications.

THE NETWORK OF UNIVERSITIES

But we are not yet done. There are further layers above the administration and the alumni. Consider the overall scale of universities, including colleges, that compose the system of institutions invested in fundamental research and education in the United States. This is where the surprises emerge. Here we find the real sources of the strengths of universities. And this is where we most clearly see knowledge advancing. Within the network of universities, the "field" is, as it were, the gulf stream that sets the intellectual weather and even the climate.

There are almost six thousand colleges and universities in the United States, if you include all institutions, with roughly even amounts of public and private nonprofit institutions. Among all of those, there are approximately seventy universities that are classified as "leading research universities." Along with a number of small, elite liberal arts colleges, these institutions set the standards of excellence for the mission of higher education. The dual system of public and private universities has many interesting features to it, but for our purposes there are not significant differences.[4]

In other words, there is no great difference for faculty whether you are at a public university or a private one. I have spent my career almost equally at both, and I can attest to the proposition that your life as a scholar is the same. What you focus on and what you aim to achieve is the same. One might say this is one of the glories of the U.S. system. Public universities such as the University of California, Berkeley, the University of Michigan, and the University of North Carolina are absolutely of the same level of academic distinction as the leading private universities.

How does the academic world operate at the national level? There is very little coordination or collective action among these institutions, as institutions; there is a very high level of competition at the middle level (schools and departments between universities competing for faculty and students); and there is a huge amount of coordination and collaboration at the bottom, at the faculty level.

Most people do not realize this is the case. They think universities are organized into groups, such as the Ivy League or the Big Ten, and some may be aware of national organizations like the Association of American Universities. They think university presidents can meet and decide to do or not do various things: Do more work on climate change. Or forge an alliance that would generate more cures for diseases. And so on. But this is not possible. The "collective organizations" such as the Ivy League are really athletic conferences. When Ivy presidents gather to discuss whether to increase the number of football games annually, they may also talk about common issues in the academic realm. But no joint actions are ever on the table or taken. And the national organizations like the AAU really just provide opportunities to meet and discuss matters of shared interest. Yes, the organizations will lobby on behalf of their members on relevant congressional legislation and administrative regulations, but little more is done at this level.

At the level of schools and departments (law, business, medicine, history, literature, chemistry, and so on), the situation is quite different. Here there is, as mentioned, an ongoing and intense competition for hiring and retaining faculty and for both undergraduate and graduate students. The primary life of a dean or chair is to retain and recruit faculty, which entails endless discussions and pleas and persuasion. The relative standing of your school or department is of critical interest to everyone, and you live in a universe of explicit and implicit rankings that matter significantly. As imperfect as each ranking may be, it is nonetheless a fact of life that every single school and department carries around with it a pretty solid working idea of just where the school or department stands relative to others.

We now return to the level of the faculty member, the professor. If you are a professor, your world is very much created by the people who are your peers at all of the other institutions, especially those who work in your field. Although a professor of Civil War history, for example, may be very valuable to his or her department, very few colleagues would share that specific expertise, even though they might all be excellent historians. This is why each professor needs relations with faculty elsewhere. And this is true for almost all scholars.

Those at your own institution are your colleagues, and you will interact with them a lot by sharing drafts of papers and manuscripts, discussing ideas, thinking about teaching, and so on. But the bulk of your "colleagues" will be made up of similarly situated faculty at all the other universities across the country and, in many cases, around the world. This is your "community" of fellow scholars and teachers. Together the members of this community will make up the "discipline" in which you work, sponsoring the journals in which you will publish, creating the lectures you will be invited to deliver, setting the standards for what work is to be honored, and all in all making up the culture in which you will exist as a scholar and teacher. They will be the people who serve as the "peer review" for your grant applications, your journal submissions and book manuscripts, and they will be the ones who write blurbs for your books, invite you to deliver distinguished lectures, recommend you for awards for your academic accomplishments, and organize the festschrift for when you retire.

Even though you are formally a member of the faculty of your university, you nevertheless will be looking for approval from your colleagues at *other* universities. They will be the ones who have the power to affect your life and career, much more so than the colleagues at your own institution. Although your own colleagues in your university will make decisions about your professional life (for example, to be granted tenure, promoted or appointed to a professorship), that decision will be influenced by, if not determined by, what those colleagues at other universities say about you.

Your shared interests as well as your career are determined by forces outside your own institution. The centrifugal forces within the university are made exponentially stronger by the linking of faculty with other faculty around the country who have the same academic interests. It is not in any sense hyperbolic to say that most often, faculty care more about that community than about their own community or institution, even if they care a great deal for the latter.

Your primary community as a scholar goes beyond your own institution, which is secondary. You share your identity with both. The community, though, is where the ongoing conversation about your field, your knowledge, happens. This community is extremely hard to create, and it is where knowledge preservation and generation happens.

No other sector of society is organized along these lines. The knowledge creation fostered by the university system is ongoing, alive, organic. It is not static. You join your institution to become a member of this wider community of fellow scholars. There is no governance of this system overall. Harvard could not be Harvard without the rest of the system. No one stands above it all, above the system; there is no president of higher education, who says you should do this part and another person should do that. So, we have both a vertical community and a horizontal community, and in the modern world that feature is unique to universities.

There are important qualifications. Faculty members share the interests of their school and department, and more broadly their university, in maintaining the institution's quality and standing. And there is a public spiritedness in most faculty when it comes to building the immediate community of the university. But still, faculty naturally look to their national, and international, compatriots for intellectual engagement and recognition.

THE STUDENT

Every faculty member has had the following thought, in consolation for the fact that one's scholarly achievement is invariably smaller than one had hoped at the outset: "Well, whatever lasting impact my scholarship has, which may be minimal, I at least have had a positive, and even for a few profound, impact on the lives of many of my students." And for the students themselves, what they want most is to be in the company of talented people who have spent their lives trying to understand something of high value and importance. Caring about one's subject is just as important as knowing about one's subject.

Students are the lifeblood of the university. There is genius in having the ranges of generations present, from the newest and youngest to the most senior. You live and work and study in a community that represents the full spectrum of life experiences. It results in a continual freshness, an eagerness, an openness, along with an intellectual parenting role that forms bonds for life.

The teacher-student relationship can be as deep as almost any other in life. It is a privilege to be able to introduce and witness the development of young people following in the path of the generations before and in your own path.

As for the student, they have an opportunity that will almost certainly never come again, the chance to be in an environment that sustains and nurtures a devotion to the greatest ideas and works of human expression. This immersion will bring the student to a point of understanding that will last a lifetime. And the student is the beneficiary not of a single professor but of a discipline, of the network of universities and the work that they have collectively generated, and this will be transmitted to the student through the professor standing at the front of the classroom. The student is taught by the network, by the system, not by a single professor.

And you, the student, are called upon to be creative in

the same way as everyone else on campus, even though you have far less life experience and academic training for such creativity.

If and when students approach this calling with eagerness and sincerity, they will be able to improve their powers of thinking, to figure out why one's capacity for comprehension may not match one's own expectations or the capacities of others. And the student will realize one of the greatest phenomena of education, namely that the more you know, the more you can appreciate how much more there is to know. To learn is to have the doors to the world open up to you. It is an unfortunate fact about our minds that they naturally seek to simplify everything. I like to tell my students to try to learn to make every serious problem as complex as you possibly can.

One of my favorite stories is from early in my teaching career, when a senior faculty member said he had passed by a student speaking privately to a professor who, listening carefully, finally said: "But have you considered . . . ?" That, he said, and I agree, is the essence of a great education.

I know all this sounds overly positive, perhaps even utopian. But when the question is posed, I believe the vast majority of students today would affirm the power of the educational experience they have received.

The on-the-ground interactions between students and faculty, and between students and the university, are direct and candid. As mentioned above, every professor faces the end-of-term student evaluations for their course. And there is no holding back by students in the criticisms (and praise) they have to offer. Whether those are made public is one question, but I have never known a faculty member who did not take them seriously.

The chance to shape the future while rethinking what we think we know is a vital benefit of having to teach students. Again, it is difficult to teach, far more so than almost anyone realizes. In that process of preparation and classroom performance, faculty relearn for themselves what they are trying to convey. The comments and reactions of the students themselves will also change your expertise. For the professor, teaching is a way of teaching yourself about what you're teaching.

THE SHARED MISSION

The modern American university system figured out how to enlist some of the most talented young people of each new generation to devote their lives to exploring the realm of human thought and inquiry and to create a shared community of like-minded people across the network who will collectively augment the whole. The sum is greater than the individual parts, creating that utterly vital sense of having a shared mission.

It is a singular structure—more of a loose confederation (with some need to tighten here and there) than a strict hierarchical organization, yet filled with subtle constraints and intangible rewards that combine to create a highly effective community—Tocquevillian in its balanced equilibrium of forces. Give your "employees" a guarantee of lifetime employment *and* a norm of deference and even autonomy over their basic assignments of research and teaching. Then have a system of multiple universities that are separate and discrete and highly competitive in the middle range of their structures and independently collaborative at the level of the professors. Even the press, which probably is the closest to universities in terms of essential structure and organizational elements, does not work in this manner. The entire journalism department within a company does insist on a degree of "independence" from the business ownership, on a theory that the journalists must be able to cover the news free of potential bias. But the editors assign stories to be reported on to the reporters, who do not have the freedom to cover what they choose, how they choose (or, at least, very few do). Nor is it ever the case that reporters have an "independent" relationship with their peers at other newspapers such that they would look to that broader community for validation about what they were doing.

On the other hand, it is unthinkable in a university for a dean or department chair (the equivalent of an editor) to "assign" a topic for research to a faculty member.

"Knowledge" is a dynamic process, and it is the *ongoingness* of knowledge that the university understands, protects, and emphasizes. It is worth emphasizing again that sometimes you don't know what you think or what you believe until you hear other people say it, perhaps via just a little difference in the way they express the idea. An ongoing dialogue is the result of the network of universities and how each one is structured. It is the purpose of the entire system.

The only structural comparison I can think of, in fact, is democracy itself. In a liberal democracy, the government has an important but limited role, and citizens are protected against government control—our prime instance being the First Amendment. They cannot be "ordered" to do this or that. They are not "employees" and have the freedom to do things with others, with fellow citizens but also with citizens of other nations as they wish. And people do. During the high tide of globalization, one of the themes for debate, both lauded and condemned, was that certain citizens were thinking of themselves more as citizens of the world, it was said, than as citizens of their home nations. Whether that is a good or bad thing is not the point here; it just is one example of the "freedom" that is extended to citizens in a liberal democracy, a freedom they cherish and defend for themselves and that can limit their allegiance to and identification with their own country.[5]

In contrast, authoritarian states are deeply bothered by citizens having such a degree of freedom to explore alliances independent of what the state wants. Such freedom is perceived as a threat, and more obedience is demanded. We in democracies say we believe that our system is more likely to generate both a stronger loyalty and a more creative, dynamic population and society. We can say the same about the university. The closest match, structurally, to the modern American university is America.

CHAPTER TWO

THE FIRST AMENDMENT

THE MODERN HISTORY OF THE FIRST AMENDMENT IS one of the great American stories. It is a story of the twentieth century, starting during and after World War I, a moment that witnessed the rise of communism and socialism as a global force. In that period, the U.S. Supreme Court launched a project of interpreting the First Amendment and the principles of freedom of speech and press that would reshape the nation and even the world. What we today take for granted—that free speech and free press are fundamental to a free society, a good society, and a good life—was created over the ensuing decades in a range of cases that collectively gave us a jurisprudence unmatched by any nation before or since.[1]

That jurisprudence has shaped modern identity and become a central element of daily life. Freedom of speech is not only a constitutional doctrine about the limits of official censorship but also a cultural norm. Every time we confront an opinion we dislike and the idea pops into our head that maybe we should let it be, that's the First Amendment at work.[2]

Not a day passes in the contemporary world when some great question is formulated, at least in part, as a free speech question. For a scholar of the First Amendment like me, there is an endless series of actual issues and cases from which to create relevant hypotheticals for my annual classes on what free speech means. We are barely even conscious of the fact that almost every major issue at any given point in time becomes in one form or another a "First Amendment problem." Many other nations, especially democracies, stand in awe, and often puzzlement, of the centrality of free speech in our lives. But free speech is not only a law, or a doctrine, or even just a constitutional principle—it is part of the essence of what it means to be an American. It instructs us how to live and think and interact in the public arena and about what we ultimately value. It touches on the very ends of life.[3]

The words of the First Amendment are deceptively simple: "Congress shall make no law abridging the freedom of speech ... or of the press." The Bill of Rights, where this freedom came first, was not added to the Constitution until 1791, four years after the Constitution was ratified in 1787. Over the centuries, many people have attempted to discern exactly what the Framers may have understood these words to mean. This has not brought forth much illumination. Today, the elaborate, even labyrinthine, doctrinal structure of the First Amendment we have developed is far beyond anything even hinted at in the world as it existed in the eighteenth century. Even the most fervent constitutional "originalists" have participated enthusiastically in making this happen. If you were to search through all of the Supreme Court precedents on the First Amendment, you would find only a handful of sentences directly referencing what the Framers of the Constitution wrote or said about the intricate issues we regularly face and have to resolve in cases before the courts. I say this neither critically nor dismissively but only as a simple fact about the limits of the help we can hope to receive from the historical record on details of doctrine.[4]

And, yet, if we move from the specifics to the general intellectual atmosphere in which the Constitution and the Bill of Rights were drafted and adopted, there is much that can be said. This was the period of the Enlightenment, when ideas of reason, objective truth, and scientific experiment took hold, in opposition to centuries of religious dogma. And there is no question, as so many have noted, that Enlightenment thinking affected how former colonies went about structuring a government and a society. In fact, America became the practical experiment for these grand ideas: to lodge sovereignty in the citizens and not the government, to follow the principle of limited government, to build a state with several competing branches of authority, and so on. And, as we will see, the grand ideal of free speech and a free press touched questions of how to think about the role of reason and objectivity in exploring the world.[5]

So, when the first three First Amendment cases finally landed together on the doorstep of the Supreme Court in 1919, the justices faced a problem of first impression but had a deep well of thought to draw on from across many centuries, including ideas formulated by such notable figures as John Stuart Mill (in the nineteenth century) and John Milton (in the seventeenth century). The issues before the Court were both simple and hard: When can the government stop a speaker from advocating for illegal actions by an audience? When can the government forbid and punish speech critical of established government policies because others may be induced to resist compliance? This issue, of the scope of protection under the First Amendment for "subversive" speech, became the core around which the entire jurisprudence evolved. And the answers were not self-evident: Why in a democracy would you ever want to protect speech that seeks to upset or overturn the legitimate decisions of its citizens? Why would you want to protect those who would unfairly attack other citizens and seek to exclude them from full rights in the democracy? Why would you want to protect speakers who would seek to mislead other citizens? Why would you want to protect speakers who would, if successful, overturn free speech itself?[6]

The answers given to these questions would become the basis for providing further answers to just about every other issue of free speech to come. As that picture of the First Amendment emerges, we can then see how the parallel development of the modern university merged with the First Amendment into a single, grand, American project.

THREE CASES

The three cases—known as *Schenck*, *Frohwerk*, and *Debs*—all involved defendants who agitated against American involvement in the war in Europe. They were each prosecuted under the Espionage Act of 1917, which made it a crime, during times of war, to "willfully cause or attempt to cause insubordination, disloyalty, mutiny, or refusal of duty, in the military or naval forces of the United States, or . . . willfully obstruct the recruiting or enlistment service of the United States, to the injury of the service or of the United States."[7]

Charles Schenck was one of several individuals who handed out pamphlets attacking the mandatory draft, or conscription. Jacob Frohwerk wrote for a small German newspaper in Missouri that expressed opposition to America joining the war against Germany. And the most interesting of the three cases, *Debs*, involved Eugene Debs, the leader of the Socialist Party and a candidate for president of the United States. He had given a speech in Ohio in which he also opposed the war and praised individuals who had refused to be drafted. (While in jail for this speech, Debs received over a million votes in the presidential election of 1920.) The question posed in these cases was profound for any democracy: When can criticism, however harsh and strident, of government policies, however important to the society (for example, drafting citizens and going to war), become a reason for the government to intervene and censor the speaker?[8]

The results in the Supreme Court were not an auspicious beginning for the principle of free speech. The justices unanimously rejected each defendant's claim of First Amendment protection. The author of all the Court's opinions was Justice Oliver Wendell Holmes, Jr.[9]

Holmes embodied the tensions that lay at the foundation of free speech. He had served in the Civil War and been severely wounded at Antietam. He knew from experience the mindset of a nation at war, which has and needs a certainty of belief about the rightness of its cause. There is no such thing as the open-minded soldier—and, beyond the soldier, we all have to make choices in life, and beliefs are necessary to choose. But as one of the foremost intellectuals and legal scholars of his time, Holmes also understood the need to reject simple-minded, unreflective convictions and to learn habits of skepticism and openness to new ideas and new truths, because that was how knowledge and civilization have advanced. These tensions lie at the heart of life.[10]

In *Schenck*, Holmes wrote that it might be true that "in many places and in ordinary times the defendants . . . would have been within their constitutional rights." But not in this place and time. Presenting a clear instance where "censorship" would be allowed, Holmes famously said: "The most stringent protection of free speech would not protect a man in falsely shouting fire in a theater and causing a panic." The question, Holmes continued, "is whether the words used are used in such circumstances and are of such a nature as to create a clear and present danger that they will bring about the substantive evils that Congress has a right to prevent. It is a question of proximity and degree." Holmes postulated that the context in which the defendants spoke created excessive risks for the nation: "When a nation is at war many things that might be said in time of peace are such a hindrance to its effort that their utterance will not be endured so long as men fight and that no Court could regard them as protected by any constitutional right." A "clear and present danger," Holmes concluded, could be inferred by the jurors in the trial court from the general circumstances in which the words were spoken.[11]

In *Frohwerk*, as well, Holmes wrote for the Court that the newspaper's clear opposition to the war could have resulted in a listener or reader being persuaded to resist the call to fight. He said: "[W]e must take the case on the record as it is, and on that record it is impossible to say that it might not have been found that the circulation of the paper was in quarters where a little breath would be enough to kindle a flame and that the fact was known and relied upon by those who sent the paper out."[12]

Finally, in *Debs*, Holmes continued this theme of permitting the jury to infer that "the words used had as their natural tendency and reasonably probable effect to obstruct the recruiting service." With Debs—a presidential candidate— receiving a ten-year prison sentence for his words in a public speech, the Court's rejection of his claim for protection under the First Amendment highlights in the most vivid way possible the distance between the free speech sensibilities in the nation and the judiciary in that moment, and what they shortly became.[13]

Indeed, Holmes soon shifted his perspective on how to think about freedom of speech (why he did so is a subject of extensive speculation). Later in 1919, he suddenly became a heroic advocate for free speech. In *Abrams v. United States*, several Russian immigrants in New York City expressed their opposition to the United States entering the war, not because they were opposed to fighting Germany but rather because they believed the war was just a pretext for suppressing the Communist Revolution in Russia. To protest, they called for a general strike of workers, including at munitions factories. They, too, were prosecuted under the Espionage Act of 1917, which was expanded by the Sedition Act of 1918 to also make it a crime, through "utterance, writing, printing, publication, or language spoken, [to] urge, incite, or advocate any curtailment of production in this country of anything or things, product or products, necessary or essential to the prosecution of the war in which the United States may be engaged, with intent by such curtailment to cripple or hinder the United States in the prosecution of the war . . . ." The majority of the Court continued the entirely "reasonable" view of free speech created in the earlier trio of cases and upheld the convictions. Holmes, however, now with a new perspective, offered a different theory of the cases and wrote the most compelling, commanding, and spellbinding defense of free speech ever made.[14]

Now in dissent, Holmes did not start by noting that the

right of free speech cannot possibly protect all speech. Rather, he began by telling us how unnatural it is for us to want to be tolerant of speech we fear and hate. What is "reasonable" to us because it's "natural" should, in fact, be rejected in favor of more considered perspectives on how we should behave. Here is Holmes on what is "normal" for human behavior:

> Persecution for the expression of opinions seems to me perfectly logical. If you have no doubt of your premises or your power and want a certain result with all your heart you naturally express your wishes in law and sweep away all opposition. To allow opposition by speech seems to indicate that you think the speech impotent, as when a man says that he has squared the circle, or that you do not care wholeheartedly for the result, or that you doubt either your power or your premises.[15]

Intolerance is our natural state of mind. We do not naturally approach life in order to learn and increase our knowledge. But we must master that intellectual skill, even if it's not easy to do so. Free speech will help guide us there. Holmes continued:

> But when men have realized that time has upset many fighting faiths, they may come to believe even more than they believe the very foundations of their own conduct that the ultimate good desired is better reached by free trade in ideas—that the best test of truth is the power of the thought

to get itself accepted in the competition of the market, and that truth is the only ground upon which their wishes safely can be carried out.[16]

Now, insofar as Holmes is saying that we should believe as "true" whatever the "marketplace of ideas" decides is true, he is not necessarily persuasive. There is a classic debate about how to accept the value of "truth" and yet live with what we believe to be "false." There are also legitimate questions to ask about what constitutes "truth" and its relation to understanding and knowledge. But these puzzles are not necessary for us to resolve here. What is important is that Holmes was taking a very strong position in favor of tolerating speech far beyond what our natural impulses would dispose us to do. As he saw it, choosing this course is a critically important decision rooted in basic values of reason, objective "truth," and knowledge. It is ultimately about the meaning of the Constitution, as well as the ends of life.[17]

As Holmes then put it, practicing the intellectual modesty and self-doubt that, he claimed, results from having erred in the past:

That at any rate is the theory of our Constitution. It is an experiment, as all life is an experiment. Every year if not every day we have to wager our salvation upon some prophecy based upon imperfect knowledge. While that experiment is part of our system I think we should be eternally vigilant against attempts to check the expression of opinions that we loathe and believe to be fraught with death, unless they so imminently threaten immediate interference with the lawful and pressing purposes of the law that an immediate check is required to save the country.[18]

Even though Holmes's opinion was a dissent, his account of freedom of speech became a lodestar. It remains the benchmark to this day. It established the architecture for the modern First Amendment. Reflecting on what the Enlightenment had bequeathed to future centuries, Holmes articulated a theory of the First Amendment that has appealed across generations, beginning with his own.

What is so notable about his analysis was the acknowledgment that the First Amendment is not meant to reflect what is "reasonable" to us, in the sense that it should merely implement our natural inclinations. The "logic" of intolerance is what comes naturally. By contrast, the "logic" of tolerance is the result of examination of our tendency to err in how we approach thoughts, ideas, and opinions. Free speech, as we now conceive it, is counterintuitive, and that makes it hard to live by. Moreover, we embrace this self-restraint because of our interest in a higher value or end—we want to expand our understanding, our knowledge, our truth, and our capacities to engage in that pursuit. (Here you might see one of the origins of what I earlier called the scholarly temperament in the university context.) The First Amendment puts us, as it were, back in a wilderness of ideas and behaviors, where we are forced to rely on our wits and hone skills we need in our normal lives.

The Constitution and the Bill of Rights established the limits of government. In the case of freedom of speech and press, they limited government's power to censor. But what happened, beginning with Holmes's dissent, is that the technical question of the limits of government could be answered only by developing a conception of how to live. It's no wonder, therefore, that the First Amendment and free speech became not just another legal doctrine but ultimately part of what it means to be an American and what it means to establish a good life.[19]

Soon, Holmes was supported by another famous jurist, Louis Brandeis. In *Whitney v. California* (1927), the state of California prosecuted a woman under the state's criminal syndicalism act, which prohibited, among other things, "organizing" or "knowingly becom[ing] a member of, any organization" advocating criminal syndicalism. Criminal syndicalism included "any doctrine or precept advocating, teaching or aiding and abetting . . . unlawful acts of force and violence . . . as a means of . . . effecting any political change." The defendant had attended a convention of the Communist Labor Party where some members voted for a platform calling for overthrow of the government (which the defendant opposed). Brandeis authored a concurring opinion joined by Holmes. The result was another world-making statement of the meaning of free speech. Of particular note was Brandeis's characterization of the intolerance within each of us. Noting that "[m]en feared witches and burned women," he wrote: "It is the function of speech to free men from the bondage of irrational fears." Echoing Holmes, he developed the theme that fear is what drives us in the first place and that we need courage to replace it:

Those who won our independence by revolution were not cowards. They did not fear political change. They did not exalt order at the cost of liberty. To courageous, self-reliant men, with confidence in the power of free and fearless reasoning applied through the processes of popular government, no danger flowing from speech can be deemed clear and present, unless the incidence of the evil apprehended is so imminent that it may befall before there is opportunity for full discussion.[20]

Brandeis, like Holmes, was alert to the emotions that lead us away from the path to knowledge, and even from reality itself, and take us in dangerously harmful directions.

Soon the Holmes and Brandeis idea of free speech would rise from a dissenting view to the prevailing view of the Court in a succession of cases strongly supportive of the free speech and press rights of citizens.[21]

But Holmes's and Brandeis's views did not simply win out. In the years immediately after World War II and extending into the next decade, rising fear and intolerance in reaction to communism led to a backlash against free speech. It is not overstating things to call it an episode of national hysteria. Of course, there was an active reality underlying these fears, as the Soviet Union expanded its authoritarian control over neighboring countries, maintained a bellicose stance toward the West, and had spies in the United States. In retrospect, however, the level of fear in America and the actions taken as a result were vastly disproportionate to the real threat, both externally and internally.

We all know this as the McCarthy era, after Joseph McCarthy, a U.S. senator from Wisconsin, who leveled extreme and reckless denunciations at individuals who were suspected of having any ties to or sympathies toward communism. When the United States arrested and prosecuted the leadership of the Communist Party in the United States on grounds of conspiring to overthrow the government, the case—*Dennis v. United States* (1951)—reached the Supreme Court. The majority of justices accepted the government's view and rejected the claims of the defendants that their rights to organize and speak were protected by the First Amendment.[22]

In an opinion that would come to be regarded by many as a concession to government-enforced intolerance, the justices put aside the clear and present danger test in favor of a more fluid one that sought to balance the gravity of the danger against the likelihood of it happening. This new test was thought to be more relevant and appropriate to large conspiracies—fostered and supported by foreign nations—that might make it harder for the government to prepare to stop the resulting harms. To the majority of the Court, the clear and present danger test might be useful when the speakers are small groups of protesters, with nothing more than pamphlets and megaphones in hand. But an international, highly disciplined, and organized effort to bring about the destruction of the nation is quite another matter. Surely, the majority reasoned, the public and its government need not have to wait until just before the "putsch is about to be executed," when in reality it would by then be too late. Such a sinister and subterranean movement led by an enemy nation could reasonably be thwarted before it reached that irretrievably dangerous point. This, at least, was the view of the majority, and so the convictions were upheld and the First Amendment claims denied.[23]

Soon after the hysteria of McCarthyism passed, the excesses of the period came to be seen in retrospect, by most Americans, as the equivalent of "fearing witches and burning women," to borrow from Brandeis. It became yet another lesson from history of our susceptibilty to out-of-control intolerance. Now, jurists and other Americans saw that the First Amendment had to be interpreted to be extremely protective of speech in order to provide a buffer against those future moments when we would inevitably, and collectively, lose control.[24]

In the late 1960s, the Court recovered the sensibilities of Holmes and Brandeis and pronounced the final judgment on the First Amendment and how to deal with speech that incites illegal conduct. *Brandenburg v. Ohio* (1969) concerned a small group of the Ku Klux Klan gathered in a rural part of Ohio. Members of the group brandished firearms and spoke of taking "revengeance" against Black and Jewish people. A local television station was there to record it. As offensive as this speech was to most Americans, the Court held, the First Amendment shall protect speech unless it is "directed at inciting imminent lawless action" and was "likely to induce such action." The bar for the government to restrict speech was now again set extremely high.[25]

Case after case has since cemented this concept. *National Socialist Party of America v. Village of Skokie* (1977) involved a group of neo-Nazis marching in Skokie, Illinois, a city made up of thousands of survivors of German concentration camps and, overall, a large Jewish population. *Snyder v. Phelps* (2011) involved a religious group that protested the funerals of servicemen and servicewomen for being part of a government and society that had violated God's laws. In both cases, the demonstrators prevailed, helping to solidify the modern notion of free speech in America.[26]

In the almost half century since *Brandenburg*, Holmes's and Brandeis's views became the dominant framework. It asks a lot of us. It is not an easy thing to do or to live by. We must live with the most reprehensible ideas, really until they are about to become action. We do so because we care about knowledge and truth, and because free speech represents our commitment to use the tools of reason and dialogue to achieve the equilibrium between order and values we believe in. Freedom of speech, then, is about overcoming our impulses to excessive intolerance in order to hone our capacities to better seek knowledge. In the discrete realm of official censorship, we commit ourselves to extraordinary tolerance, extraordinary self-restraint, not because that is how all life should be but because we want a meaningful example of how to rein in natural tendencies that undermine our higher goals.

THE JURISPRUDENCE

With this framework in place, subsequent jurisprudence filled in the spaces. Once the clear and present danger test of Holmes and Brandeis became the standard, it was no longer routinely eviscerated by notions of deference to judges and juries, who often shared the intolerance of their fellow citizens. The result was that speech, no matter how noxious, would be shielded from censorship until the government could prove that it had no other option at hand to prevent serious illegal and harmful consequences. A wide range of doctrines combined to create a free speech regime in a society now ostensibly willing to confront speech of all kinds.

Well before *Brandenburg*, in the 1930s and 1940s the Supreme Court declared that citizens had a fundamental right to bring their voices to the public realm, including public spaces, like streets and parks. Courts could not enjoin future publication of a newspaper only on the basis that it had been found to publish "malicious, scandalous, and defamatory" content. Aggressive and unpopular groups such as the Jehovah's Witnesses could set themselves up on city sidewalks to play their Victrolas with records denouncing Catholics and seek adherents among the passersby. People had a right to pass out leaflets with political messages in public areas even though that might well lead to litter and costs to city services in cleaning up afterward. Anyone could go door-to-door with their political messages even though many residents did not welcome them and thought it an annoying intrusion.[27]

Decisions in the 1960s and 1970s expanded protections considerably. This was an era of huge upheavals in American society: the civil rights movement, the anti–Vietnam War movement, the women's movement, the environmental movement, and others. There were vast changes underway, and it was inevitable that the First Amendment would move to the front and center. Furthermore, the issues at stake were both transformational and could be dealt with only on a national basis. Other factors made a national perspective more important than ever: the growing economy, the emergence of the United States as a global superpower, the advent of the first truly national communications technologies (radio and television). The old world of more local control over public issues had to give way to national authority, and this meant the First Amendment would necessarily be called upon to provide national answers to speech and press issues.

The centerpiece of the era's First Amendment jurisprudence was the Court's famous decision in *New York Times Co. v. Sullivan* (1964). The case was as much a civil rights case as a First Amendment case. The *New York Times* had published an advertisement composed by a civil rights group that outlined many injustices enacted by public authorities in the South against Black people fighting on behalf of racial justice and solicited financial support for their work. The advertisement contained sharp criticisms of actions of the police in Montgomery, Alabama. L. B. Sullivan, the Montgomery commissioner responsible for overseeing the police, though not named in the advertisement, sued for damages under Alabama libel law. There were some minor errors in the advertisement's account of improper behavior, but none could reasonably be thought to explicitly refer to Sullivan or result in any pecuniary loss. Nevertheless, under the prevailing law in Alabama, Sullivan was able to file a claim in court for reputational harm, and the presumptions were in his favor. The Alabama Supreme Court affirmed a verdict against the *Times* and a large damage award for the time ($500,000). The *Times* sought review in the Supreme Court, and the Court took the case. On its face, the case seemed to reveal a vindictive judgment by a southern court and jury against civil rights advocates and a liberal northern press, involving a heretofore localized system of defamation law that could be used to punish and chill national debate about national issues. The case seemed to tee up a revolutionary decision, and that was exactly what happened.[28]

The Supreme Court's ruling did two novel things. First, the Court took the common law of libel—one that had been around for centuries and had been traditionally regarded as a matter for individual states—and overrode it with a national standard. The Court held that when public officials—a category subsequently expanded by the Court to include all public figures—sue for damages for falsehoods that purportedly harm their reputations, they can recover damages only when it can be shown that the statements were made with "actual malice," defined as knowing or reckless disregard of the falsity of the statements. In line with the extraordinarily solicitous posture toward free speech begun by Holmes and Brandeis, the Court declared that the First Amendment wanted a world in which speech was "uninhibited, robust, and wide-open."[29]

The second thing the Court did in the *Sullivan* decision was to root the theory of the First Amendment in notions of democratic self-government. The Court reasoned that the Constitution was written to reflect a central idea in the Enlightenment philosophy, namely that sovereignty resided with the citizenry and not with the government itself; this Madisonian conception of what a democracy means in America pervaded the framing of the Constitution. Therefore, the Court argued, the authority and responsibility of citizens to exercise self-government meant that public officials could not be permitted to sue citizens for damages or damaging falsehoods about them absent truly extraordinary circumstances—again, in essence, where it was clear that the speaker had knowingly or recklessly defamed the official. Otherwise, the Court explained, there would be a "chill" among citizens as they debated the issues of the time, especially since some misstatements are inevitable in public debate, given the passions public issues often elicit. Many citizens would find it just too dangerous to step forward and speak if the consequences of a misstep were so severe. The Court also noted that public officials (and public figures) have ample means to counter the alleged falsehoods if they chose to do so. Hence, in the Court's view, the balance of interests favored a result that seriously limited the ability of public officials to seek redress through the courts to protect their reputations.[30]

The more proximate source of the idea of tying the First Amendment to the exercise of self-governance in a democracy was a lecture delivered in the late 1940s by a philosopher and college president named Alexander Meiklejohn. In the lecture—later published as a small volume entitled *Free Speech and Its Relation to Self-Government*—Meiklejohn rejected Holmes's idea that the First Amendment embodied a general mission of seeking truth and proposed instead a more limited notion that it was only about the exercise of self-government in a democracy. The classic image of the New England town hall represented for Meiklejohn what the First Amendment was all about—citizens coming together to collectively address questions about the governance of their polity.[31]

The Court's decision in *Sullivan* was widely understood as embracing Meiklejohn's vision, even though the majority made no reference to him or his work. Yet it is also true, importantly, that as of this writing the Court has never embraced Meiklejohn's *rejection* of the search for truth rationale when it has pronounced on freedom of speech and press. It is critical to see free speech in the context of the political system and the exercise of self-government. But it would be wrong to limit its reach to that role alone. It's not that notable speech about literature and art, for example, would necessarily be excluded from protection. The only influential scholar who has taken that extremely limited notion of free speech was Robert Bork, a fact that played a role in his failed confirmation hearings in 1989, when he was put forward as a potential new Supreme Court justice. (I was part of the U.S. Senate hearings on the Bork nomination and made this point about his First Amendment scholarship.) Meiklejohn himself rejected the idea and contended that all speech relevant to political judgment, which would include art and literature and philosophy and so on, should be protected.[32]

The error of Bork's, and Meiklejohn's, view has to do not only with the reach of protection but the reasons for the protection, too. Art, literature, and so on should be protected fully for their role in expanding knowledge, the ultimate goal of the First Amendment, above political self-governance. As such, then, the working assumption in the jurisprudence is and has been that *both* truth and democracy are core values represented in the First Amendment.

New York Times Co. v. Sullivan set the stage for other cases that further expanded the boundaries of the First Amendment in the modern era. There was *Brandenburg v. Ohio*, as we've seen. Another case worth noting is *Cohen v. California* (1971), which involved a challenge to government claims that highly "offensive" speech could be prevented, and that this was consistent with the First Amendment.[33]

Paul Robert Cohen was in a public courthouse wearing a jacket with the words "Fuck the Draft" written across the back. Upon entering a courtroom, he took off his jacket. An officer arrested him, and he was charged under a California statute prohibiting offensive conduct that "disturb[ed] the peace or quiet of any neighborhood or person." The Supreme Court held that the speech was protected by the First Amendment, with Justice John Marshall Harlan II writing the opinion for the majority. A conservative, Harlan offered a very forceful defense of free speech, illustrating an important fact about the evolving jurisprudence of free speech in America—it has been the consensus among both liberals and conservatives that we should have an expansive definition of free speech and press. Harlan rejected California's argument that it was reasonable to disallow certain highly offensive words such as the word "fuck" in public settings. For the Court, this was an analytically impossible approach to free speech. As Harlan wrote in his majority opinion: "one man's vulgarity is another's lyric." Harlan powerfully observed, too, that every word in every context has a discrete meaning, and as a consequence it must be recognized that to excise a word is to excise ideas, an act that under the core First Amendment values is unacceptable. Finally, and most important, the majority was unmoved by the claim that a state should be able to protect its citizens against being confronted with deeply offensive speech when they go out in public. To the Court this was something we had to learn to live with.[34]

Several other cases insisted that public authorities protect speakers against hostile audiences, even when the speaker was helping contribute to tensions and in some cases potential violence. One such free speech case reached into the hallways of our public schools. In 1965, thirteen-year-old Mary Beth Tinker wore a black armband to school as a sign of protest against the Vietnam War. Officials said she could not bring this controversial political protest into the school. The Supreme Court of the United States agreed with Mary Beth, declaring that "freedom of speech or expression [are not shed] at the schoolhouse gates." Having to confront speech you may view as dangerous or offensive is a principle in America that goes all the way down to junior high school.[35]

The trend continued into the 1980s and 1990s. In *R.A.V. v. City of St. Paul* (1992), for example, the majority opinion (authored by Justice Antonin Scalia) held that the state cannot single out racist "fighting words" for prohibition.

And in *Virginia v. Black* (2003), the Court narrowed the powers of the government to ban cross burning only to situations
where there was a proven intent to intimidate specific persons,
or so-called true threats.[36]

This, then, is America's version of freedom of speech and
press. It has taken a century to unfold, but we now have a rich
tableau of decisions that is clear and cogent. Again, the artists
who have put this picture together are from all sides of the
political spectrum and of very different judicial philosophies.
Of course, there have been arguments in opposition to this
consensus from both ends of the spectrum, and there are some
intimations from the current Supreme Court that certain features of this picture might be changed. But the basic system
of freedom of expression is entrenched, and the "free speech
century" is an extraordinary tale.

HOLDING THE CENTER

The jurisprudence of free speech allows for, if it doesn't actively
create, a rather raucous society. Which prompts the question:
What conditions must exist in a society for this system to
work? And how will a society with such a system hold on to a
center that most of us want?

The fact remains that the collective life we have created
for ourselves through the First Amendment is not one that is
going to be easy to abide by. Your reputation, your sense of
vulnerability to physical and other injuries (especially if you
are already part of a minority group whose members have his-

torically been the victims of discrimination), your sense of fear that you may be accosted in public settings by ideas you find deeply offensive—these and other very reasonable concerns are magnified by modern First Amendment law. It cannot be said too many times: The First Amendment is hard. Not only does it run counter to our natural impulses, as Holmes pointed out, but also the harms that follow from the choice to take the principle to these extremes are not trivial.

Every other democracy in the world works with a much narrower conception of free speech.* Our jurisprudence is more refined, more extensive, more elaborate, more robust than any other country's, but that does not mean it's right or preferable to the approach in other societies where the principle of free speech takes more "reasonable" dimensions. It does not seem right to hold that other nations with more moderate free speech regimes are less "democratic" than the United States.

So we must ask again: What are the conditions necessary for our highly particular version of free speech to work out well? We cannot elide the reality that under our regime, we have to live with a lot of highly dangerous and offensive ideas that any moral or ethical person should reject: advocacy of

---

* It is instructive here to look at Germany. Since the end of World War II, Germany has hewed to a cardinal principle that speech advocating Nazism should never be protected; quite the contrary, it must be prohibited. The thinking behind this approach is perfectly obvious. The sense that the nation has a special susceptibility to the Nazi ideology or that it may be perceived as having such a vulnerability is so great that in this particular case "tolerance" would truly signify acceptance, or an appeal, or even a flirtation. History makes the condition necessary or at least understandable.

murder, of invidious discrimination against vulnerable groups (Black people, Jews, women, and so on), of hatred and viciousness against others, of the denial of civil rights (including free speech itself), and of dangerous falsehoods likely to mislead even those who are not normally gullible. We have stripped ourselves of the capacity to intervene and reestablish standards of decency and morality. This is a system in which society is left with no legal checks on speech that disrespects others, urges violence, revels in misinformation and falsehoods, propagates stupidity, or forsakes ideas and norms we all should value. Some might reasonably ask: Should it hardly surprise us if our society splits apart, with the extremes crowding out the center and leaving us standardless?

To use the terms that Holmes offered us in his opinion in *Abrams*, when he said "that the best test of truth is the power of the thought to get itself accepted in the competition of the market": What is that "market"? The more the "market" is composed of elements we can trust, the more we should be prepared "to wager our salvation" on this conception of free speech.[37]

Clearly, one would say there must be a certain level of education and intellectual capacity for a population to succeed in such an open environment. What more?

We should be thankful that we have at our disposal multiple means of private censorship that can help bring the Wild West of the First Amendment under civilized control. We shall see that private censorship, which is by definition beyond the scope of the First Amendment, is a necessary condition of living a reasonable life but also allows for the biases that Holmes identified as inherent to human nature—in other words, the same biases that lead to excessive official censorship also lead to excessive private censorship.

By "private censorship," I mean the many ways we have to exercise pressure and censor bad opinions and bad speech and bad speakers. We can shun, condemn, cancel, and so on. We are always calling out intolerance, or calling out bad speech, or changing the words we can use, or shifting things into moral categories, or this or that. We need some private censorship to make life livable. On the other hand, we don't need other private censorship that would make life unlivable. These are the intricate and complex judgments inherent in social life.

We need a center, and we need institutions that hold that center. We need a good moderator, with good values, and a serious capacity to think well, with respect to expertise, to help lead and guide the discussion.

What does a moderator look like? It looks like the press, and, I will argue, it also looks like the university.

In virtually every Supreme Court decision holding that "bad" speech must be protected, the Court's opinion has made sure to indicate that the justices view this bad speech as bad. Holmes himself was unqualified in his mockery of the speakers he was protecting with his high-minded ideas about the meaning of free speech. In one case, he referred to the speakers as "poor and puny anonymities." In other words, built into the jurisprudence of free speech is the reassurance that there is a center. These cases frequently involve prosecutions against people at the margins of the society—immigrants, in particular—and the justices' reactions indicate their disgust with the rabid intolerance directed toward defenseless and supposedly insignificant people. The real concern of the Supreme Court has been the problematic minds of the intolerant rather than the value of the expression protected.[38]

Yet reassurance goes only so far. The idea that there has to be a center became at least implicitly part of the constitutional analysis with the evolution of the press. Over the course of the twentieth century, the press, or mass media, moved increasingly toward the center in American public life. Before that it was more part of the contentious extremes—partisan, extreme in opinions, inflammatory, what was known as "yellow journalism." Yet early in the 1900s, a more "responsible journalism," and a certain professionalism, emerged. The story of the press in the twentieth century has two primary parts, one being print media and the other being broadcast media.[39]

The first is of the daily newspaper in American life. The twentieth century saw a steady march toward monopolization of daily newspapers in cities and communities all across the country. By the 1960s, more than 90 percent of cities in the nation had only one daily newspaper. This special status produced many things, but one in particular was the rise of a sense of responsible journalism—objective, nonpartisan reporting of the news. At the same time, the profitability of these enterprises increased significantly, which made it possible to scale up newsrooms, establish foreign bureaus to cover international news, and expand the coverage into areas such as the arts and sciences. In the 1960s and 1970s, daily newspapers were the primary forum for public discussion of public issues and also the source and reflection of shared community values. The idea of the press as the fourth branch of government began to take hold.[40]

The Supreme Court decisions of this era codified this status with a number of very favorable decisions. It is perhaps no coincidence that the epochal case of *New York Times Co. v. Sullivan* involved America's leading newspaper. Another of the seminal First Amendment cases of this time was *New York Times Co. v. United States* (1971), otherwise known as the Pentagon Papers case. Here, the two leading daily newspapers in the country, the other being the *Washington Post*, were involved. Each had received surreptitiously from a government source (who was later revealed to be Daniel Ellsberg) copies of the seven-volume history of the Vietnam War that had been secretly commissioned by the Department of Defense as a means of better understanding how that disastrous war happened. The newspapers informed the government that they had the Pentagon Papers, and indicated that they were planning to publish some portions deemed to be newsworthy in satisfying the public's right and need to know. The government responded by asking U.S. district courts to enjoin publication. This was one of the few times in U.S. history that the federal government had sought to prohibit a newspaper from publishing information. Unsurprisingly, the case took an expeditious journey to the Supreme Court for a definitive ruling.[41]

The Court ruled in favor of the press, holding that, under First Amendment doctrine disfavoring "prior restraints" on speech, the government was precluded from calling on the courts to stop publication without demonstrating the most grave and irreversible dangers—something equivalent to the publication of the dates and times of the sailing of a transport ship in a time of war. There were numerous opinions by the justices, with various qualifications and ambiguities about the full extent of the protections being afforded to the press. But the actual decision on the merits, however potentially limited in scope, was enough to turn the case into a landmark of First Amendment law.[42]

Allowing chaos to prevail over order, the Court was ready to set up a contest of equals between the government and the press. The government has a legitimate interest in maintaining secrecy in the conduct of national and foreign affairs, reflected in an elaborate system of classifying information as "secret." But the government also overdoes it on the secrecy business and cannot always be trusted to exercise this power properly. The press stands as the institution capable of countering the risks of government abuse of secrecy and is a worthy representative of the public and its interest in knowing. Hence the rules of the contest handed down by the Court: the press has no right to any secret or other information, and the government can take whatever steps it wants to protect against disclosure; but if the press is otherwise receiving such information, even from a government employee acting illegally, it may choose to publish it subject to certain limits involving grave public harms. As the great constitutional scholar Alexander Bickel observed at the time, the Pentagon Papers case created an adversarial relationship between the government and the press. In doing so, the Court recognized the profoundly important systemic role of the press in the functioning of American government and society.[43]

After this decision, a debate began among First Amendment scholars and within the press about the idea of the latter enjoying a special standing under the Constitution. The press is not some ordinary for-profit business selling a product but a unique institution with a systemically important status and committed to acting to advance the public good. Some turned to the "press clause" in the First Amendment as signaling that special standing. In 1975, Justice Potter Stewart wrote a notable law review article in which he advocated for this interpretation.[44]

The debate has continued to this day. Several Court decisions have resisted claims from the press for unique rights above what would ordinarily be recognized for the public. In *Branzburg v. Hayes* (1972), a grand jury investigation into criminal activity that had been reported on by the press led to the state demanding the press reveal information in its possession about its sources. The Court refused to grant a special privilege against revealing that information, although there was one very important potential qualification that might matter under certain circumstances of prosecutorial abuse. The Court also rejected granting the press special access rights to government-controlled spaces and information, holding that the press has no more rights than the public.[45]

Still, the fact that the question about the standing and role of the press in America under the First Amendment is still a live one in itself makes it so, to a significant degree. There is no doubt that journalism as a whole, as a profession, has benefited from and been shaped by this potential high status.

The second part of the story of the press in the twentieth century is radio and then television. Early on, the fear that these powerful new media would be taken over by extreme and dangerous forces led to the enactment of comprehensive federal legislation designed to moderate and control that private power. The Communications Act of 1934 established a federal agency, the Federal Communications Commission (FCC), and charged it with the allocation of licenses to broadcast and to regulate the licensees, all according to the general standard of serving the "public interest, convenience and necessity." Soon the FCC created a "fairness doctrine" requiring broadcasters to cover controversial issues of public importance and to do so reflecting multiple viewpoints. Here, too, the government helped create the center.[46]

It wasn't until 1969 that the Supreme Court got around to answering the question whether this government intervention was constitutional under the First Amendment. In *Red Lion Broadcasting vs. FCC*, the answer was a resounding and unanimous yes. The Court found nothing to object to and indeed even intimated that the regulatory regime designed to maintain a responsible public role for new media may have been constitutionally mandated, not just tolerated. The thesis was that private control over this new and important means of communication was far too dangerous—the unmediated control of this powerful new medium could jeopardize the public interest in fair and full discussions of public issues. Given the physical confines of the electromagnetic spectrum, only a few licensees would emerge and would have too much power to go unregulated.[47] Yet as we have noted, the traditional "press" of daily newspapers was also monopolized by private owners. Should we not have similar fears when it comes to the newspapers and feel reassured by government regulations? Just a few years later, in *Miami Herald v. Tornillo* (1974), which involved a state statute compelling newspapers to offer a right of reply to political candidates criticized in the paper, the Court unanimously rejected the idea—noticeably without ever mentioning *Red Lion* or the broadcasting model. Here, any government intervention was to be feared, and Americans needed to appreciate that "editing is what editors are for."[48]

Now, one might say this was just an anomaly in the Court's decision-making. It ignored the issue of the comparable levels of monopolization of the two parts of the media and failed to explain the need for a consistent approach. But I have always thought the Court's apparently incongruous decisions revealed something wiser: The traditional press, newspapers, were well into the process of developing professional standards, which was not necessarily the case with broadcasting. The uncertainty about how the still-nascent medium would develop if left entirely to the free market was reason enough for public controls designed to keep it close to the center of public opinion. And the permission to regulate broadcast media could, and I think did, have a positive effect on the print medium, by providing an example of what might happen if it were to become irresponsible. Meanwhile, the true autonomy and independence of print journalism would provide a check on government excesses in regulating the newer medium. This was decision-making based on how a system works best, rather than an insistence that everything similar must be treated similarly.[49]

Yet over the past several decades, regulation of any kind has fallen out of favor. In the 1980s, during the Reagan administration, free-market ideology gained force and political favor. Government regulation was out and private markets were in. That shift largely ended the regulation of broadcasting under the FCC. By the end of the decade, the commission had all but abandoned the fairness doctrine and other regulations. Cable television emerged. Although the typical American city had only one cable company operating dozens or hundreds of channels, many people, including judges, focused on the sheer number of channels as a sign that public regulation was unneeded. The withdrawal of regulation yielded the hyperpartisan channels that we know today.[50]

Then came the internet. It was hard to understand at the beginning just how revolutionary this new technology would turn out to be. But it eventually became apparent that every single human being could become a "publisher." To many, the prospect of a true "marketplace of ideas" had been realized. To help fulfill this dream, Congress enacted the Communications Decency Act in 1996. Under Section 230, every "provider" or "user" of an "interactive computer service" was insulated against any claims of liability that would normally fall upon a "publisher," such as a newspaper or broadcaster.

This effectively removed any risk for owners of platforms such as social media companies, giving them the full freedom to pursue business models aimed at maximizing the volume of content—regardless of its potential social harm—and keeping users engaged for as long as possible by feeding them more of what their initial behavior suggested they want (exactly what Holmes would describe as normal but problematic).[51]

Over the next two decades, the world of mass communications changed in ways and to a degree never experienced before in human history. Everyone from scholars to ordinary citizens who try to monitor and limit their children's access to this new world are still struggling with the effects of the transformation.

Some of the effects are already manifest. One is the sharp decline of the traditional media, notably the daily newspaper. The press was once the only game in town when it came to communicating with the public. But the internet created other opportunities for reaching an audience. The business model of newspapers (and broadcasters) that had been so successful for decades evaporated. As we now know, with the benefit of hindsight, traditional publishers and journalists compounded their problems by failing to imagine a world where people would prefer reading the news on a screen to reading a printed version over breakfast. Newspaper after newspaper closed up shop or went through a restructuring that left them hollowed-out versions of what they had been. Only a billionaire could potentially save some, as with hallowed publications like the *Washington Post* and the *Los Angeles Times*.

The great achievements of professional journalism were dismissed by many who welcomed the end of its presumptuous voice of authority. Today, the "responsible" institutions of journalism are fighting for relevance, and an audience, in a vast ocean of text and video and talk.

Another consequence of the internet was the evisceration of public responsibility. Some tried to force owners of social media platforms, through law or new norms, to exercise the kind of responsible editorial controls that had long been important to the traditional press. The *New York Times* or the *Washington Post* would never knowingly accept a political advertisement, for example, that contained a material falsehood, whereas owners of social media platforms were unconcerned about distributing such falsehoods. The profound suspicions of any government regulation, at every level of society, including conservative justices on the Supreme Court, made the notion of regulation unappealing at best. Furthermore, there was no consensus across the political spectrum of the kind that would be needed for legislative interventions in favor of content-moderation requirements, which some liberals favored but conservatives opposed believing such policies were a means of "censoring" their voices.[52]

It appears that the new internet publishers will be successful in casting themselves as the successors to the newspaper editors of old; that is, they can make their own choices about what to "publish," and it is their First Amendment right to do so. The liberal and conservative justices on the Court today seem to be uniting around this constitutional outcome.[53]

For years now, the press has been in decline as the center in American political and social life. To so many of us, it feels as though the extremes have overtaken the center.

THE FREEDOM OF THE UNIVERSITY

The First Amendment affirms that our society is dedicated to the value of knowledge and to the search for truth. In the twentieth century, leading jurists, aware that our natural tendencies make us less open-minded than we should be, placed stringent limits on government censorship and demanded that we tolerate extreme speech and ideas. But for the First Amendment to continue to work, at least three things must happen. First, our society must embrace the value of knowledge and the search for more of it. Second, we must learn the lessons about our bad tendencies and work to counteract them. And third, using all the techniques at our disposal (other than government censorship) for organizing our collective discussions in the most beneficial and productive ways, we must find and hold the "center."

We have seen how the Court has tried to identify and hold the center, most notably by extending special recognition to the traditional press. While there have been ongoing and intense debates about the extent to which the press should be granted a special standing under First Amendment doctrine, the concept of the press as "the fourth branch of government" persists in constitutional philosophy and, to an extent, in society generally. Now with the internet and the rise of new forms of communication that have broken down the institutions of the press and the philosophy of professional journalism, the press has a declining role in establishing and holding the center.

This is where the university comes in.

For all who wonder about the standing and role of universities in society, the First Amendment is the necessary context. Universities are fast becoming the last surviving, or at least most vital, institutions that are consistent with the purposes of the First Amendment and necessary to its continuous realization. Even more than the press, I believe, universities *accomplish* the First Amendment, as it has been defined and as it has evolved. Collectively, which is how we must think about it, universities make up a massive system with extraordinary effects on millions of people. They are dedicated to abnormal openness and thus serve as an intermediate layer between the First Amendment and its extreme openness on the one hand and the broader society on the other, where the hard complexities of belief, insistence, openness, and tolerance must arrive at some livable equilibrium. They create—and exemplify for American society—a model of dialogue focused on the desire for knowledge and bounded by the scholarly temperament. Nearly twenty million students who attend colleges and universities every year are exposed to this mentality, along with the countless other citizens who interact with these special institutions.[54]

Like the press, universities are an independent voice fearlessly pursuing truth. They are thus in need of protections, since in performing their role they will inevitably find themselves in conflict with government authority and even societal opinion. They are not built to fight in the political arena, and they are vulnerable to retaliation and demands for submission.

The university is most like the press (the press of old, at least) in that it is both the fulfillment of the purpose of the First Amendment and one of the conditions that make the First Amendment possible. The Court should make itself a guardian of the university, and whenever the government seeks to meddle in its affairs and to bring it under control, the Court should demand that the government step back or provide the highest level of justification—a compelling state interest—for any such intervention. The university should be part of the idea of a fourth branch of government. The text of the First Amendment provides for freedom of "the press" as well as "freedom of speech," and it would not be an interpretative stretch to include the university into these powerful and significant phrases. The university now plays an almost identical role as the press in American society: We should think of "the press" as institutions dedicated to generating and informing the public about important knowledge (across the entire spectrum, from science to the arts to political and social life) and which follow professional standards of inquiry (journalistically and scholarly). In other words, we should think of "the press" as having a functional rather than a colloquial definition and meaning.[55]

In certain respects, the Supreme Court has already arrived at such recognition for universities. In First Amendment jurisprudence, there are a number of significant references to universities as being entitled to constitutional respect.* In a well-known opinion in *Sweezy v. New Hampshire* (1957), two of the leading justices of the twentieth century, Justice Felix Frankfurter and Justice John Marshall Harlan II, concurred in a decision of the Court to protect a guest lecturer at the University of New Hampshire, Paul M. Sweezy, against an expansive and sweeping investigation by the state attorney general into Sweezy because of the series of lectures he delivered. The basis of the investigation was a fear of the professor's alleged links to communism. Frankfurter and Harlan, both in the moderate to conservative traditions of judicial philosophy, recognized academic freedom as a core constitutional interest and offered the following caution, no doubt mindful of the damaging impact on academic life of the Red Scare of the 1920s and the McCarthyism of their own time: "Scholarship cannot flourish in an atmosphere of suspicion and distrust. Teachers and students must always be free to inquire, study and to evaluate."[56]

Justice Frankfurter then warned of the "grave harm resulting from governmental intrusion into the intellectual life of a university." Citing a statement by scholars at two "open" universities in South Africa, Frankfurter and Harlan proclaimed words that have resonated ever since: "It is the business of a university to provide that atmosphere which is most conducive to speculation, experiment and creation. It is an atmo-

---

* For an in-depth analysis of academic freedom–related jurisprudence, see DAVID M. RABBAN, ACADEMIC FREEDOM: FROM PROFESSIONAL NORM TO FIRST AMENDMENT RIGHT (2024).

sphere in which there prevail 'the four essential freedoms' of a university—to determine for itself on academic grounds who may teach, what may be taught, how it shall be taught, and who may be admitted to study."[57]

Other decisions of the Court reflect a recognition that universities deserve a special solicitude. *Keyishian v. Board of Regents* (1967) involved New York law and regulations that required faculties to sign a certificate denying links to communism as a precondition to teach. The Court held: "Our nation is deeply committed to safeguarding academic freedom, which is of transcendent value to all of us and not merely to the teachers concerned. That freedom is therefore a special concern of the First Amendment." Yet it is true, as distinguished constitutional scholar Robert Post has observed, "judicial references to a constitutional concept of academic freedom have been largely vague and rhetorical, with the result that 'no clear doctrines have emerged.' We simply do not know what the constitutional status of academic freedom might be. When confronted with constitutional questions of academic freedom, courts have typically turned instead to generic First Amendment principles of freedom of speech."[58]

The strongest recognition of the special role of universities under the First Amendment has, in my view, come in the affirmative action cases, where the question has been whether universities could consider race as a factor in deciding whom to admit as students. In several decisions, the Court acknowledged that universities deserved substantial deference in making these judgments, even in the highly charged and fraught context of using race as a basis for public policy, something otherwise strictly forbidden ever since the Fourteenth Amendment was added to the Constitution in the aftermath of the Civil War and the end of slavery.

As Justice Lewis F. Powell, Jr., wrote in *Regents of the University of California v. Bakke* (1978), "Academic freedom, though not a specifically enumerated constitutional right, long has been viewed as a special concern of the First Amendment. The freedom of a university to make its own judgments as to education includes the selection of its student body." Powell then cited Frankfurter's "four essential freedoms" in *Sweezy*. He went on to reference *Keyishian*, saying that "[o]ur national commitment to safeguarding of these freedoms within university communities was emphasized in *Keyishian*."[59]

Powell continued: "The atmosphere of 'speculation, experiment and creation'—so essential to the quality of higher education—is widely believed to be promoted by a diverse student body. As the Court noted in *Keyishian*, it is not too much to say that the 'nation's future depends upon leaders trained through wide exposure' to the ideas and mores of students as diverse as this Nation of many peoples."[60]

Even the most recent university decision of the Court in *Students for Fair Admissions, Inc. v. President & Fellows of Harvard Coll.* (2023), in which the conservatives on the Court joined together to reject the earlier affirmative action precedents like *Grutter v. Bollinger* (2003), still left the door at least slightly ajar to universities to justify use of race—a position they would not be likely to have extended to any other institution.[61]

The idea that universities have this special standing is, as with the press, not a fully developed doctrine in the jurisprudence of the First Amendment. The press is the closest analogy, as I have indicated. There is still much left to fill in. Yes, the "press" is explicitly mentioned in the language of the First Amendment, and universities are not. But consider the difficulty of defining who is "the press" today, in this new world of the internet and universal publishing. One could argue that the university plays something closer to the role of the press, as it was conceived in the eighteenth century, than, say, various digital channels that might claim the mantle.

Universities are a version of the press but offer deeper inquiry into public issues and are always on call to serve as a check on government and society. If their deadlines are far longer, the scope of their work and remit in pursuing truth reaches everyplace where knowledge may be secured and advanced. Universities are places devoted to the widest fields of human discovery, never limited by what may be newsworthy at any given moment. And, as many have noted amid the Trump administration's clawing back of federal funding for universities, the results of academic research and discovery have benefited society in more obviously utilitarian ways, from curing disease to cracking the atom to creating technologies that have powered our economic dynamism and enhanced our quality of life. But we need not and should not see merit in universities only where there are tangible benefits. To know, to find truth, and then change our minds and find truth again—that is the mission of the university and of life itself.

Even if the Court were for some reason not to hold that universities are entitled to special protections under the First Amendment, that is not, and should not be, the end of the matter. The Supreme Court decides only the limits of government censorship (in one form or another). But society may also decide that the Constitution—in this case, the First Amendment—endorses or establishes certain principles. Principles or norms can become influential even without any official enforcement; consider the power of many taboos.

The defenders of the university should be seeking this less formal constitutional dimension, too, as well as the formal doctrine of the First Amendment. As we have seen, the inclusion of freedom of speech as a fundamental principle enshrined in the First Amendment and then interpreted so rapturously by the Court not only set up a constitutional barrier against certain government actions with regard to "speech" but also created a norm. That norm has entered into peoples' minds and shapes our lives generally, as individuals and as members of society—having a kind of extraterritorial effect. Think about how often someone will say that some act is a violation of their free speech rights, even when that is not technically true. These instances should not be mocked—though often should be challenged—but rather seen as a sign of how powerful the principle is in American life, above and beyond any strictly constitutional questions.

It is up to us, in other words, to protect the university amid the attacks it is currently facing and those it will surely face in the future.

CHAPTER THREE

THE FIFTH BRANCH

WE NOW HAVE A THEORY OF THE UNIVERSITY. IT derives from the evolution of both the First Amendment and of the system of universities over the past one hundred years. These by now distinctly American institutions are aligned in mission—the quest for knowledge—and share a deep understanding of how our natural instincts are problematic for pursuing this purpose and how, through constant effort and practice, we learn to bend toward seeking truth. This is the primary lesson of the extraordinary regime of the First Amendment, and it is fulfilled in a very specific, and very successful, way by the network of universities and their complex, fit-for-purpose, and irreplaceable design. Universities provide solid support for the center and, accordingly, make the modern First Amendment possible. Yet the character of the university, created to foster the pursuit of knowledge, is also highly vulnerable and in need of protection.

In 1915, a foundation for the concept of academic freedom was established in The Declaration of Principles on Academic

Freedom and Academic Tenure of the American Association of University Professors. It, too, emphasizes the virtues of the collective university search for truth according to professional scholarly standards and norms. I very much like the strong and generally healthy spirit of independence that comes with the idea of academic freedom. But we can now add critically important features: The freedom of the university is rooted in the bedrock of the nation's constitutional framework. There is nothing vague and indefinite about this claim. The university is one of the key layers (along with the press) in the overall structure of the nation and broadly designed to advance the quest for better understanding and truth, a hallmark of the American ethos. Not just part of the fourth branch, universities represent a fifth branch, as essential as the press to our collective life and success.[1]

This is a fraught and urgent time for the university and, indeed, for the entire country. The university as a major national institution is under attack. What will happen in the years and decades to come? Universities are not alone in this situation, but they must preserve their integrity, and we all have a responsibility to protect their standing in our democracy.

IDENTITY

Everything starts with how we think of the university, from within and without. As is so often the case, the most important first step is a mental one: shaping how we understand who we are and where we stand in relation to others. The more substantive we can be, the better. A spirit of independence is already fairly strong among faculty and universities, but we need to reinforce it and then put it into practice.

Those of us who are denizens of the university should think of our institution as part of the constitutional structure of the nation. The university is built into our foundational ideals and sheltered accordingly. This is no small matter. Given recent events, I cannot help but think about this truth in the context of university leaders responding to intrusive questioning by a hostile congressional committee. When members of Congress make demands on universities to punish certain faculty or to challenge academic decisions, one's answers should depend on what is an appropriate line of questioning and underlying agenda against a national institution that constitutes the fifth branch of the nation. How the press or how Supreme Court justices respond when they are challenged would be an appropriate guide.

The simple fact is that leaders at every level, from faculty to deans to presidents to trustees and alumni, must focus now on building this sense of mission. We must express this over and over again, taking every opportunity to explain and affirm it in as much detail as possible. This idea cannot be treated as something that everyone will grasp on their own, or will naturally intuit. Like the modern meaning of the First Amendment itself, the idea of the freedom of the university is not self-evident, and the latter is certainly not part of the general knowledge of faculty, students, and the public. We must never be shy about characterizing the university as one of the key means of realizing the human need to know, to understand, and to search for truth. It must be repeated endlessly and with all the infinite variations that will come over time.

Each person will use words and analogies that are slightly different, and each time the particular shading will add to the overall idea and make it a little more real and secure. The principle is about a system, not a "right" held by any single professor or university. This is an important feature that needs emphasizing in itself. We spend far too much time these days trying to distinguish individual institutions from others, feeding that competitive spirit that has many positive features but is secondary to the needs of the collective whole. The role of the university, broadly conceived, must be fortified in our minds and the minds of the public. We should have more voices across the full spectrum of colleges and universities saying just that.

Students need to be brought into this vision from the moment they arrive on campus to graduation. I have often been in meetings and conversations about how to get students to realize early on their responsibilities to give back once they are able, so that the next generation may succeed like them. These "student/alumni development" discussions are valuable. But I have never heard a comparable discussion on the idea that every student be informed about the larger societal role of the university and all that accompanies this standing. In our current environment, we spend an inordinate amount of time educating students in the history and identity of their own discrete college or university to instill that sense of loyalty and pride that is part of the process of creating a community.

We would be wise to spend as much time educating them on the nature and sources of the mission of the university and the deep substance underlying it.

Similarly, this principle should be part of the process of selecting all leaders of the university, namely chairs, deans, provosts, and presidents. To do this would significantly increase the likelihood that the mission and the identity of the university will naturally be incorporated in all decision-making and all representations made by universities. Whenever people are considered for these roles, the first question they should be asked is how they would articulate their views of the freedom of the university.

Finally, boards of trustees should also be composed of individuals who are in alignment with the academic mission and the fundamental principle of freedom of the university. As I mentioned earlier, maintaining the appropriate role of boards in general academic life is both complex and fraught with concerns of overstepping. Having in mind the very special nature of the university is critical to maintaining the proper balance.

Of utmost import, all members of the faculty must understand that they have a responsibility to live by and uphold their role in this concept of the university. We are not talking about some individual privilege of each professor but rather the right of a system, of a network, of a collection of people who have accepted a role in a larger body. We are part of a whole, and it is the whole that provides the mission, the terms under which we pursue the mission, and the basis for the standing we have in the society.

Finally, we need major figures—leaders from every sector of the society—to speak to this role. We have become very good at describing the benefits to society that result from the translation of basic research in science and engineering. But this familiar account lacks the richness of the principle I am talking about here. There are "benefits" of all kinds brought by the university, not least from the arts and humanities that bring us to a better grasp of life in every single dimension we can imagine. It is a mistake of misrepresentation when we describe and defend the university with respect to only a limited number of its many branches of knowledge or when we talk merely of the economic or health benefits that follow from advances in basic research.

We must also avoid and reject certain existing and corrosive ways of talking about universities. We should cringe when we hear anyone, including those on the inside, speak about the university as a business. Nothing is more harmful to the meaning of universities than when students are depicted as "customers" or "throughputs," or when there is seemingly serious talk about "credentialing" students or about certain areas of the university being "profit centers," or when people focus on increasing "efficiencies" in the "transmission of information." This is one of the most pernicious characterizations of the university, and it should be scorned in every form.

Money is crucial to the freedom of the university and also poses a threat. We have become far too dependent on sources of income that create risks to the fundamental mission. Philanthropy is now a critical piece of the financial base. Even public universities have moved in this direction. Traditionally, the primary source of funding for these institutions has been from the state. But public universities have suffered in recent decades as state legislatures have cut back. Most have tried to make up for this by accepting more out-of-state students, who are charged a higher tuition, and by an increasing emphasis on securing donations. For private universities, which generally have very low if any state funding, private donations have always been a focus, but that emphasis is becoming more urgent every year. And, as everyone has now learned as a result of the Trump administration's attacks, the other source of public funding, for universities public and private, has been federal dollars coming primarily from the National Institutes of Health and the National Science Foundation.[2]

There is a dynamic here that creates risks to the freedom of the university. Universities are forever growing. This is true for multiple reasons. Some have to do with the competitive structure of these institutions. Each year, every university puts huge effort into recruiting and retaining faculty and students. The result is a steady increase in expenditures for salaries, research funds, housing assistance, benefits, financial aid, improved residential facilities, and better amenities all around. But growth is also the result of an institution committing itself to the desire for knowledge. Virtually every new discovery opens up new possibilities for increasing our knowledge, and typically that means more faculty in more space with more things that facilitate that inquiry and teaching more students. In other words, as new tributaries of knowledge are opened up, you need more people and more capacity to explore them. Technological advances add to the pressures to build out our institutions. While I was president, I worked with the understanding that research universities expand at the rate of one million square feet every decade, and sometimes even double that rate.

Universities, even those with large endowments, live by a thin budgetary margin and do all they can to fulfill their mission responsibly. And this is why they are especially vulnerable to retrenchments in financial support.

With funding from the federal government, traditionally there has been a system of "peer review" that serves as a guarantee that grants will be aligned with academic values and opportunities. Faculty from around the country serve on panels to sort out which applications to accept and which to reject. This system has worked extremely well for the past seven decades, more or less. There have been times when policy directives led to an emphasis on some goal, such as more focus on finding cures for diseases rather than simply basic research. But these directives from on high have generally been consistent with academic principles.

When it comes to private philanthropy, the situation is more complex and difficult. In my experience, very few donors seek to invade the academic space. They understand, even if only vaguely, that the university is a self-governing institution following academic values and that those must be respected. What is taught, what is researched, and so on are sacred areas of academic choice. There is no doubt that by allowing donors to give gifts to certain programs or aspects of the institution, you are, in effect, permitting those to be favored over others. But it is then up to the university itself to use the funds that had been allocated to these areas to be distributed elsewhere and achieve a proper balance. In any case, everything depends on the leadership exercised by the chairs, deans, and president in preserving the integrity of academic decision-making, which is why it is so critical, as I indicated in chapter one, that these individuals are steeped in these values and have the character to see that they are protected.

But we must bear in mind that the risks are not only in the decision about a gift and what it will support. The additional question is who sits at the table of decision-making more generally, and there is always the possibility that major donors will be afforded an inappropriate role. This threat is often invisible even to those within the institution, and that makes confidence in the leadership all the more important.

One solution would be to make it a condition of every gift that a slice of the donation be allocated to a "freedom of the university" (or "academic freedom") fund. This type of condition is regularly imposed, so it would not be a completely novel concept. And it would do two very important things. It would help educate and impress upon everyone the fundamental principle, and it would over time build up a quite substantial amount of money to support the defense of the principle. Even better would be if all universities pooled these funds to be used collectively when needed—as, for instance, in response to threats and attacks from a presidential administration.

I have to confess that when I was a university president,

I never thought about the need to build a reserve of funds that would serve as a cushion or protection against efforts to use the leverage of money to interfere with academic governance. In retrospect, this was a mistake. Now, as we witness authoritarian interventions into the workings of the university, it seems imperative that universities stash money away to lessen the power of that form of leverage. This will require time and self-control. It is true that endowments are a form of protection, providing a guaranteed base of funds for necessary expenditures. But there is a common misunderstanding about the flexibility of uses of endowments. Even with very sizable endowments, nearly all of the billions of dollars are legally tied up for specified purposes such that there is no way to draw on these funds to compensate for those taken away for malign reasons. What we need is an academic freedom rainy day fund, as it were.

Related to the money problem is the problem of athletics. As I know from my experience as a president in the Big Ten, there is simply no escaping the fact that big-time athletic programs long ago took on a life of their own, and the university and its leaders have lost significant control. I personally would put myself among those who enjoy college sports, but I do so with a lot of guilt. I have no doubt that what we have today is the product of fans, including alumni, as well as profit-making organizations—and not the academic or intellectual institutions themselves. And while athletics can bring good feelings—if your school is winning—much of what athletics now represents runs counter to the idea of the freedom of the university. I do not see a realistic means to reverse course in the near term. The supporters of college athletics should at the very least be instilled with some (more) regard for the special role of the university in America.

THE AUTHORITARIAN THREAT

We are living in a new age of authoritarianism. It is not, so far, the same style of authoritarianism that Europe experienced in the 1930s and 1940s. It is a softer version. The basic goal of the new authoritarianism, from the point of view of the autocrat and his minions, is to intimidate and silence the opposition just to the point that they cannot prevent you from convincingly winning every election. The pretense of abiding by the rules and norms of democracy and of basic rights and liberties is part of this version of authoritarianism. You need not cast your exercise of power in raw terms of authority, demanding obedience and submission. Rather, everything you do is presented in terms of high (democratic) ideals: protecting true free speech, ending discrimination, insisting on diversity of thought, and cleansing the society of traitors. Repression in the name of noble values is calibrated to chill speech enough to weaken but not destroy the opposition.[3]

As we have seen so often to be the case in the history of free speech, authoritarians target marginalized individuals and groups who do not have broad public sympathy, who exist in some limbo status where the ambiguities about their rights make it easier to scapegoat them. Immigrants and undocumented people can be kidnapped off of the streets or out of their homes and sent to the archipelago of holding stations and prisons, beyond the reach of their lawyers or the need for explanations. All this casts a pall over dissent. And it's done in the name of serving higher national interests.

This softer but still effective form of authoritarianism arises from a democratic election, which produces a kind of veneer of legitimacy that makes it difficult to quickly mobilize the opposition. Those who might make up the opposition struggle to understand what is happening. Is this just politics as normal, requiring normal methods of organizing for the next election? Or is this the moment political theorists since Plato have warned is the Achilles' heel of every democracy: the clever and sinister use of the forms of democracy to destroy it? Once in power, it is shockingly easy for an authoritarian to undermine democracy. You capture the other branches of government and employ the massive power of the state to breach the norms of self-restraint and curtail the opposition, and you're basically done.

There are three major theories for explaining why American democracy is in a precarious state. The first is a story of macroeconomics. Over the past half century, the United States has moved, and has been moved, toward a more laissez-faire economy. This is a prime example of the triumph in public policy terms of academic theorizing, in this case about the ideal economic system. These ideas, many of which originated at the University of Chicago, found expression not just in domestic political economy but also in the international system of trade and investment, manifesting as the so-called globalization of the free-market economic system. Other forces—most notably the easier movement of peoples and the internet—accelerated globalization.[4]

These policy choices, in the absence of countervailing moves to alleviate the costs they would bring, has led to very significant adverse results: the concentration of wealth in the very top of the income scale, the stagnation of income at the middle levels, and the increasing gap between the rich and middle-income and lower-income portions of the population. The Great Recession compounded these effects. I happened to have joined the board of the Federal Reserve Bank of New York in January of 2007, when the prevailing narrative was about the extraordinary success of the U.S. and international economy—so I had a front-row seat in watching the dissolution of the economy, with employment dropping by 8.6 million jobs lost and millions suffering as a result. Whatever the full causes of this economic and social debacle, it unquestionably led to an immense anger at the freewheeling behavior of financial and political elites, who seemed to many to have gotten away scot-free.[5]

The second theory of the current democratic demise focuses on the flaws in the structure of our political system. The phenomenon of gerrymandering of voting districts, in which one party or the other will draw districts in such a way as to ensure the success of their party and limit the potential representation of the opposing party, is one flaw. The general result is that districts are guaranteed for one side or the other and thus tend to produce candidates who are more extreme, hence making political compromise in the legislative process more difficult. Another flaw is the system of unregulated money in the electoral system due to decades of Supreme Court decisions equating money with "speech" and denying any government power to regulate so-called expenditures as opposed to contributions, which can be regulated. Because very large donors and small-money donors tend to come from the extremes, a functioning democracy becomes more difficult. This flaw also fosters cynicism among many citizens about the unfair influence of wealth.[6]

The third theory is that the internet broke our politics. The ways in which people now receive information, their vulnerability to disinformation and manipulation by sources national and foreign, and the unwillingness of the new media owners to come to grips with this reality have resulted in a failure of public discourse leading, in turn, to a failure in our government's capacity to govern.[7]

My goal here is not to provide a complete analysis or to present the case for or against the validity of individual arguments or theories. It is rather to say that each theory is a plausible explanation for what we are seeing happening today, and to some substantial degree each must be accurate. And that means the conditions underlying the current state of affairs, and the resulting threats to universities that we are now witnessing, are unlikely to dissipate soon or to be resolved easily. Donald Trump may be a once-in-a-lifetime political figure, but as many have pointed out, he is at least as much a symptom as he is a cause. The concerns we have about the vulnerability of universities and the question of how we think about their place in society are serious matters for the long as well as the near term. One thing, at least, is clear: The forces described above have centrifugal effects. Which makes the university, as a countervailing force shoring up the "center" of American opinion and life, all the more critical to the future of this country.

HOW AUTHORITARIANS ATTACK
THE UNIVERSITY AND DEMOCRACY

In every society that has fallen to, or embraced, this modified authoritarianism, the state goes after the press first and then closes in on universities next. Typically, the assault begins by undermining the leaders of the universities and then replacing them with individuals who will be more compliant. We have seen this in Turkey when Recep Erdoğan moved to secure his power, and the same occurred in Hungary, with Viktor Orbán's brutal confrontation with the Central European University.[8]

The first and most important item on the authoritarian agenda is to turn public opinion against the regime's opponents. The prime illustration here is the repeated statement that the press is "the enemy of the people." Journalists are continually charged with propagating "fake news." Vice President J. D. Vance has extended this language about "enemies" to elite universities.

Authoritarians denounce anyone who opposes them. People who have litigated against the current U.S. president are castigated as having "weaponized" the law and legal system. If you lose an election, it is declared to have been fraudulent. Anyone who supports diversity efforts for marginalized groups is said to be engaged in "discrimination" and the advancement of a "woke agenda." People who protest American (or certain other nations') policies are said to be anti-American or, worse, assisting terrorist organizations. Anyone who stands in the way of what the authoritarian and his people want will face such smears. From the authoritarian's point of view, opposition is never regarded as legitimate.

These smears often work, and authoritarians can turn public opinion, or enough of public opinion, against their enemies. Earlier we took note of how, in the nineteenth century, John Stuart Mill observed that "private" intolerance can be equally or more effective in silencing opinions than any "official" censorship. The methods for punishing people for their opinions and ideas we dislike are vast and powerful. Ruining your opponent's reputation, shunning that person, denying him or her employment opportunities—these techniques are likely to discourage most potential speakers. Then there is also private violence. Today talk to any journalist or public figure who has spoken out in ways the Trump people dislike, and you'll hear about a myriad of instances in which he or she has been the victim of threats of private violence. I myself have faced threats. The authoritarian mindset is well aware of how the mere threat of private violence can silence opponents without the autocrat needing to impose official censorship.[9]

But the most powerful strategy the authoritarian can use is

to employ the vast resources of the government in favoring or disfavoring political friends and enemies. In doing so, he relies on one of the key lacunae of the First Amendment cases dealing with this kind of "censorship." Justices have been almost exclusively engaged with how to deal with laws that directly punish or forbid certain speech, which is analytically easier than trying to determine when in the conduct of the government's business *a comparable result to that of direct censorship* should be disallowed.

Consider how the Trump administration has refused to extend security clearances or access to public buildings to law firms who have over time represented Trump's opponents— access absolutely necessary for the law firms to represent major clients. Similarly, corporations that have been viewed as in one way or another fostering political opposition or that have been engaged actively in promoting diversity have been threatened with loss of government contracts and business.[10]

As of this writing, the most dramatic instances of this strategy have been directed at universities. The post–World War II pact between the government and research universities— which saw federal funding go to advance scientific and biomedical research—has been placed in jeopardy, as the Trump administration has suspended further grants unless the universities agree to terms that threaten academic freedom and autonomy. Title VI of the Civil Rights Act of 1964 prohibits various forms of discrimination against certain groups and makes compliance a condition of receiving federal funding for a variety of activities within universities. As noted earlier, in the case of Columbia University, the administration has claimed that the university failed to protect Jewish students from discrimination on campus and has used the leverage of funding as the means of getting the university to change academic governance, put certain departments into receivership, require greater "intellectual diversity" in faculty hiring, and more. The government has taken similar stances toward universities that have favored programs and policies of racial and other diversity and, in the case of the University of Pennsylvania, permitted a transgender student to compete in women's sports.[11]

In the context of the First Amendment, these acts raise the issue referred to as unconstitutional conditions. This is a known problem, but the case law is underdeveloped. As always, there is a tension to be resolved. On the one hand, the government has "rights" just like everyone else to express its views about issues it regards as important (for example, advocating against use of cigarettes because of the health hazards), and the government has a legitimate interest in not having to fund things that might end up coming into conflict with its policies and views. On the other hand, given the vast amounts of money the government distributes, if we extend complete freedom to the state to condition contracting or funding on whatever grounds it likes—including requiring recipients to refrain from expressing certain viewpoints or ideas—then the government will be able to accomplish indirectly what the nation has already decided is a corruption of the marketplace of ideas. The First Amendment would quickly be eviscerated.

Recognizing these competing values, the Supreme Court

has intervened in various cases in the past to curtail the government from choosing this means of trying to stop certain viewpoints. It definitely should do so in response to the Trump administration, given that the threat of withholding contracts and funding is so obviously related to the government disapproval of what can only be deemed regular political speech.

Another technique employed by the administration is threatening to take action, or actually taking action, but in a limited manner that is nevertheless enough to create widespread fear. The threat itself is often enough to achieve broad silence. I am personally aware of this method, having been explicitly mentioned in certain MAGA documents as a person who should be criminally indicted as an example to other university presidents.[12]

How does fear work in society? Each day I have encountered people who privately express reservations about entering the public arena and objecting to what is happening. The reasons vary greatly: Some are fearful that something in their past will be used against them, some are afraid of becoming the target of a lawsuit, some worry about their travel and being pulled aside at an immigration checkpoint, some worry about simply being arrested, and so on. What is happening is largely invisible unless we look closely, since many people do not want to reveal their feelings of vulnerability or the fact that they are personally calculating the costs of being visibly in opposition. I believe there is far more fear and reticence than many of us might think—a fear of falling into the spreading authoritarian web, which is increasingly everywhere.

Those people I've met who are afraid of being the target of a lawsuit know that they would prevail in court, if it came to that. But they are not afraid of legitimate suits; they are afraid of spurious ones. A ridiculous lawsuit is even more powerful in its chilling effect than the legitimate one, because it indicates a readiness to use the costly mechanism of law in far more expansive ways than the law would itself allow. The fact that you will prevail in the end is small comfort against the costs of defending yourself, including your time and energy. We have seen this happen with Trump's lawsuits against news organizations. With outrageous demands for damages and clearly specious claims, the suits drag on and consume resources while threatening other interests that may be at stake. For instance, Paramount, the owner of CBS and the show *60 Minutes*, was pursuing a merger that required the sign-off of the chair of the FCC, who is a Trump appointee. Therefore, the baseless lawsuit against *60 Minutes* must be "settled" in order to achieve the business interest. Again, here, I am personally a victim of this kind of litigation. Trump has sued members of the board of the Pulitzer Prizes, on which I sat as president of Columbia, the institutional home of the prizes, for "defamation"—arising out of the award of the Pulitzer Prize to the *New York Times* and the *Washington Post* for their coverage of Russian interference in the 2016 presidential election. The suit has no chance of succeeding, given First Amendment law, but is nevertheless taking time to arrive at that result. Every action like this, however ludicrous, has the effect of spreading fear.[13]

Universities, just like is true for the press, will naturally be among the first to call out the authoritarian danger, which is in part why they will also become the first targets.

It is worth repeating that in the subtle authoritarian playbook, the techniques are always sheathed in good intentions, and actions are taken in the service of the very values that are being undermined. The face of brute force and normative rejection is rarely shown.

The upshot is that we, the denizens of the university, need to learn how to exist in such a hostile environment, one in which government (both federal and state) seems to have a malicious interest in undermining the position and credibility of the university while also helping to throttle scholarship and teaching.

THE COUNTERSTRATEGY

The question of how to respond to these new threats leads us back to the Constitution and the First Amendment. We must articulate and emphasize the notion of the freedom of the university at every opportunity. The larger challenge is to secure that principle, and the idea of the university as the fifth branch of the American system, in the Constitution.

It all has to begin with becoming much more deliberate and long term in our thinking. The analogy that comes to mind is how the civil rights movement worked so carefully over so many years, decades even, to achieve what it did in *Brown v. Board of Education* (1954). Other examples include the environmental movement or the efforts by the press in modern history to secure press freedom. You need to be careful and intelligent, and you need to plan with a long horizon.[14]

At the start of this book, I noted that in times of stress and crisis, your values—or the values you hold dear—stand out more sharply. In this sense, the authoritarian siege has done wonders for elevating academic freedom in peoples' minds. At the same time, the history of the First Amendment, as we have seen, is not one in which the courts, including the Supreme Court, have always stood up for basic liberties. Despite the heartfelt commitment after periods of intense intolerance to do better next time, the next time, when it comes, has only seen this commitment fall short. Perhaps, with the current crisis, it will be different. We certainly have had more time to refine our principles and build our resolve.

What we need is a decision or two by the Supreme Court affirming the principle of the freedom of the university and pointing in the direction of doing more. This is what happened for the press and for the idea of the press having a unique and special role to play within the American political system. Both *Sullivan* and the Pentagon Papers breathed life into the thought that the press must have special protections in order for it to perform its major role. The press seized the moment, in spite of the major ambiguities in the decisions, and has portrayed itself in that light.

What would this look like in practice? It would mean not some absolute right, as against any form of government intervention into or impact on the university, but rather a heightened scrutiny and insistence that the government meet a very high burden of justifying any such intrusion. That would be weighed against the powerful constitutional reasons for the special standing afforded these institutions collectively. In underdeveloped areas of doctrine, such as unconstitutional conditions, we would want the Court to pay special attention and to be especially alert to the dangers inherent in using funding as a lever for exercising improper controls over the university. Over time, the Court should put clear and appropriately restricted boundaries around what the government can do with this extraordinary power. No one is contending that the government cannot place any restrictions or conditions on funding, including those concerned with stopping invidious discrimination as defined by the Constitution itself. But the reach and methods of that authority must be very narrowly circumscribed, and the Court must be highly sensitive to instances of abusive intent. Consider Justice Powell's opinion for the Court in *Branzburg v. Hayes* (1972), where the Court said it was constitutional for the state to expect the press to reveal before a grand jury evidence (including its sources) relevant to criminal investigations but not in circumstances where the state prosecutor was clearly abusing that authority to punish the press.[15]

Now, it is very important to stress that all is not lost if in the end, a Supreme Court were to hold that the First Amendment will not incorporate the principle of freedom of the university along the lines of what I discussed here. There are two critical points to be made. One is that the simple debate about the idea will itself have a positive impact on how we—and here,

I mean "we" to include not just the members of the university but everyone in this country—think about the university, just as the comparable debate about the press has had on journalism. The second is that we always need to bear in mind that what the Constitution says, or provides, is not only what the Supreme Court holds to be the doctrine. We may find in the Constitution rights and meaning that are reflected there even though they cannot be incorporated into functioning doctrine. Think of free speech itself. Clearly, the Court's decisions about the scope of protection for freedom of speech have had a profound impact on how "free speech" is thought about in the society generally, how each of us embraces or incorporates the idea of free speech in our own lives, and how we then give it a meaning for ourselves, which doesn't in most instances correspond at all with the formal jurisprudence but nevertheless has an impact.

I do not know when the right moment will be or what will be the right issue for universities to make their case—it may well be right now. One reason—and an important one—to choose to litigate and go to court is that it offers the opportunity to most clearly articulate what values you are fighting for, what identity you claim, and what determination you possess to defend these principles. The Trump administration's threats to withdraw science funding from Harvard unless the university agrees to turn over major elements of its academic decision-making is truly a perfect example of unconstitutional encroachment. As of this writing, by filing its own lawsuit against the government, Harvard appears to have seized that opportunity and has now succeeded in persuading a federal judge to enjoin the government from continuing with its unconstitutional assault. But whatever ultimately happens, this path of resistance has been opened.[16]

For some public universities, that "right" is already securely expressed in the state constitution. This was the case with the University of Michigan, where the state constitution specifically confers rights of autonomy against official interference. In such cases, the principle of academic freedom is a given. But the bigger question always remains: How to bring it to life, and how to give it vitality and real force against improper interventions.[17]

Opportunities will surface with time. Here is a concrete illustration from my own experience. While I was president of Columbia, we received an inquiry about whether we might take and hold in our library the Snowden papers—millions of official documents relating to issues of national security that had been disclosed by the former NSA contractor Edward Snowden. Under the Pentagon Papers decision, there was, I believed, a very strong argument that the press—a newspaper, in particular—would be protected if it held on to these documents and then was subjected to a criminal action under the Espionage Act of 1917. In my view, if the press had this right, then universities should as well, for all the reasons I have given in this book on the parallel nature of the press and universities. In the event, we chose not to proceed with the acquisition, but this could have been an interesting case with which to establish a favorable precedent. Others will undoubtedly appear over time. It may well take years to occur, even decades; jurisprudence is usually built up incrementally. But the key point is that those who care about the university need to be thinking about this and planning for it, consciously and with serious intent.

Now, universities at this moment are most certainly facing a severe assault, and the risks appear likely to grow. I am not naïve. There is no question that when up against a determined and hostile government, it is difficult to win in the end, whatever the courts ultimately rule on the claim of academic freedom in a particular context. This is because, even with robust protections, constitutional or otherwise, the tactics of attack are almost unlimited, and the shield of principle is necessarily porous. The government can initiate investigations, file lawsuits, find ways to hold back or deny funds that seem to get around the principle. These and other actions can add up to make life unbearable and the institutional life as we know it unsustainable. In these circumstances, maintaining your sense of self and your integrity is the most important thing you can do. Strategies of appeasement never work. Concessions rarely stop further demands, and the cycle of encroachment continues. At some point sanity will return, and, if you have given up your principles and values when under pressure, you will likely never get them back or prove to others that you have.

What we need, in addition to Supreme Court cases and a broader understanding of the freedom of the university among its denizens and laypeople alike, is unity. The problem of building the capacity for collective action among universities is serious and needs to be addressed. They operate too much as autonomous institutions, even while their faculty forge extensive horizontal relationships and academic partnerships. Universities are used to competing against one another and are hypersensitive to their own institutional independence. We need to overcome that when it comes to creating the culture of shared commitment to the principle of freedom of the university across the entire system.

This is not easy, but it can be done. I saw this most vividly when I had just become president of the University of Michigan in 1997 and we were informed that we would be the next target of the anti–affirmative action movement then sweeping the nation. That movement was coming off a major victory in California with the passage of Proposition 209, which amended the state constitution to ban public universities in the state from engaging in affirmative action. The lawsuit against the University of Michigan received national publicity. There were, in fact, two cases. One involved the law school, where the policy at issue had been one I, as dean at the time, had worked with faculty to compose consistent with the latest Supreme Court opinions. The other involved the undergraduate admissions program. The law school policy was general in phrasing; the undergraduate policy, partly because of the large number of applicants to be sifted, was concrete and formalistic. It had a system of "points" that were allocated on the basis of grade averages, standardized test scores, and other criteria. It also gave a specific number of points for being Black, as well as for other races or ethnicities. This was all set forth in a "grid," which made the process very easy to grasp. At the time of the lawsuit, the grid was leaked to the *New York Times*, which published it on the front page. I remember encountering a number of alumni and others that day who were furious. Clearly, the cases did not start out well. The general environment was not at all favorable, as the California ballot proposition result showed.[18]

My strong view at the time was that the University of Michigan was far less likely to win in the Supreme Court, which is where I expected the cases ultimately to land, if this were just a University of Michigan diversity policy case. I believed that whatever the outcome, it would affect, dispositively, affirmative action policies all across the United States at virtually every college and university, since the effort to include more Blacks, Hispanics, and Native Americans in the student bodies had been regarded as a national imperative for the prior three decades. Universities were not by any means the only institutions that joined in a collective effort to overcome the history of slavery and then various other forms of invidious discrimination. Business, journalism and media, civic organizations, and even the military academies were also committed to providing more opportunities for underrepresented groups, not only for reasons of social justice but also for practical reasons of serving customers, covering issues more comprehensively, and, in the military, building an officer corps that reflected the diversity of the troops. My argument was that if the University of Michigan lost in the Supreme Court, affirmative action policies throughout the system of higher education and beyond—the great national effort to create a more just, fair, and cohesive society after decades and centuries of the opposite—would unravel. The fear was of an outcome precisely like what we are now witnessing under the Trump administration, following upon the Court's decision in *Students for Fair Admissions, Inc. v. President & Fellows of Harvard Coll.* (2023), which largely reversed the decision in our case.

I began by asking former president Gerald Ford to write an op-ed for the *New York Times* supporting the university's position. He was a graduate of Michigan and had played on the football team while he was a student. Because he was a Republican, he could lend significant credibility to the policies and the university's position. He agreed and wrote an extraordinarily powerful piece. He recounted how when he played on the team and a southern school was coming to Ann Arbor for a game, the coach of the visiting team demanded that Michigan's one Black player not take the field. The player sat out the game. That, Ford said, was reason enough for the special efforts of affirmative action to be justified and continue.[19]

Those of us defending the principle of affirmative action made personal appeals, and it soon became a campaign involving dozens and even hundreds of people trying to organize and bring about the desired result. I made a special plea to university presidents at the annual meeting of the Association of American Universities, the organization that serves the top research universities. Countless conversations followed. In the end, supporting briefs were filed by universities and the major organizations that represent them. Then we received the assistance of some CEOs of major corporations, who over time persuaded more than sixty CEOs in total to sign on to an amicus brief supporting the university. A brief by former military leaders also lending support followed and seemed to make a significant impact on a number of the justices.[20]

It is never easy being a defendant in a lawsuit, no matter how worthy the cause you are defending. In every case, there will be facts that may surface that make your case more unpopular. To join in your defense opens other people and institutions to themselves becoming a target and to the risk of being associated with someone or some institution that could turn out to be different from what you expected going in. Then there are expenses involved, in money and time. The natural impulse is to stay on the sidelines and let the litigation play out.

But organizing collective action when shared values come under attack is possible. The University of Michigan was singled out from the pack and rendered more defenseless. But the organized effort to rebuild collective support paid off.

Collective action will be the single most important factor in determining whether the freedom of the university becomes and remains a robust principle. I cannot emphasize enough how difficult it is to build a shared sense of responsibility to defend fundamental principles. And I do not for a moment want to be taken as saying that because this was done with success in the affirmative action cases it can certainly be done every time. Each attack, each principle, will bring its own issues and obstacles, as well as opportunities, and there can be no certainty that collective action will materialize, even with the most creative and persistent efforts.

Freedom of the university is a state of mind. If you are always thinking about what it means and how to fortify it as a basic principle, then you see opportunities in great controversies that you would otherwise miss. A good illustration is another controversial topic: free speech on campus.

FREE SPEECH ON CAMPUS

How universities deal with free speech is an extremely important subject on its own merits, but it is a critical question in this book, given what I see as the alignment and interconnectedness of the First Amendment and the university. The university is vital to the success of the First Amendment as it has been understood and designed. Put another way, the First Amendment could not be what it has become without institutions like the university. And, likewise, the First Amendment is vital to the success of the university. To make the point more directly, the university should think of itself as having a special responsibility to the First Amendment. To paraphrase a famous remark by President John F. Kennedy: Universities should think not about what the First Amendment can do for them, but what universities can do for the First Amendment.

There never has been a major controversy in the world that did not end up being played out on university campuses. It is in the nature of youth to feel issues passionately, and the campus inevitably becomes the location for exercising one's voice. We do not and should not see this as a negative thing. Caring about the world we live in is among the essential elements of a healthy democracy; passivity and dullness signal the very end of democracy. It is, therefore, no surprise that the profound issues in the Middle East involving Israel and the Palestinians should have landed on the university campus. But, as sometimes happens, what begins as legitimate debate and protest spilled over into unacceptable actions, including the occupation of university spaces and buildings and acts of antisemitism and Islamophobia.

We know that freedom of speech, under the First Amendment, has been designed as one context in which to learn and to seek truth. But it requires us to master certain capacities. This has been a very painful period of time for everyone who cares about every single value that has been put in jeopardy or violated. The Trump administration, as we know, has seized upon these protests as justification for a host of actions that threaten the principle of the freedom of the university, along with free speech and due process. Antisemitism has been the pretext for suspending or withholding federal grants for science and other academic activities. It is the basis on which foreign students have been arrested and threatened with deportation. And it is the basis on which universities have been summoned before Congress and other official bodies to be attacked for what has happened.[21]

But all these recent events have also been deeply disturbing to reasonable members of the university. The anger and behavioral excesses have shocked people to the core and led to deep divisions among academic communities themselves.

In this book, we have examined the broad framework of

free speech in America that emerges from a century of jurisprudence. It is an elaborate and complex system. Because the
First Amendment, like other sections of the Bill of Rights,
applies only to "state action," there is an automatic distinction
between public and private universities. The former, being
"state" institutions, must abide by the judicial decisions under
the First Amendment. The latter, being "private," are not so
obligated. (I leave aside here the difficult issues around when a
"private" institution becomes a "state" institution and the question why private universities have not crossed that barrier.)
Nevertheless, virtually all private universities have voluntarily
embraced the First Amendment as the framework for allowing
speech about public issues on their campuses.

That said, scholarship and teaching are not subject to the
ordinary rules of free speech as held by the Court over time.
For public universities, bound as they are by the First Amendment, the Court has long recognized the need to respect the
interests of the "state" in pursuing an official mission that may
necessarily entail limiting the freedom of "employees" and others. The mission of the university and the ways it is structured
to pursue that mission, even though they "restrict" speech
considerably, have been acknowledged by the Court to operate outside the normal rules that protect speech in the public
forum. So, a university can restrict speech in the classroom to
civil discourse relevant to the subject at hand or hold students
to account for making ill-considered comments or plagiariz-
ing. And the same would be true for institutional expectations
of faculty in their scholarship. But when students and faculty

meet in the "public forum" on campus and discuss and debate public issues, it's a different story. The same First Amendment rules that govern speech in the broader public forums apply to the campus of a public university, and private universities have followed suit.[22]

This means very bad and harmful speech—including ideas and opinions we properly despise, like racist, sexist, antisemitic, and Islamophobic speech—can happen and still be protected and go unpunished. As we know, this is very difficult to live with, given our natures and propensities, and given our normal and perfectly legitimate antipathy to these bad ideas. And as we have seen, important thinkers have explained why this system, as hard as it is to live by, is what we have come to accept as the best course for us as a society.

Which means, in turn, that universities should always be explaining this reality to their members and to the outside world. You need continually to describe what we have chosen to live with and the reasons for that decision. You just cannot do this enough, since the vast majority of people simply don't know what the modern First Amendment means. People may understand it in the abstract but then be surprised and shocked when they encounter it in reality.

You must also explain the limits of free speech. There are numerous exceptions—for instance, when illegal action is imminent, when true threats are made—and people should have an awareness of when they have crossed a line and moved into the area where their "speech" is no longer protected. There is no First Amendment right of speakers to engage in actions that disrupt the normal functioning of the university, whether by occupying buildings, setting up permanent encampments, or using bullhorns in the lobby of an academic building. Because there is no single word that unambiguously distinguishes between the costs of speech one must bear and those one need not, this often leads to problems both of clear analysis and public acceptance of what is happening. For example, the word I just used to describe what free speech does not cover— namely, "disruption"—might be thought to cover the pain and suffering, and resulting adverse impact on educational opportunities, of those who feel attacked by protestors expressing their viewpoints (for example, speakers yelling "From the river to the sea"), but it would not under traditional First Amendment analysis (as we have seen). People often speak of "time, place, and manner" restrictions on speech, which is a helpful phrase, too, but it also is not a bright line for making the distinctions we need. Part of what makes free speech hard is that it often involves real harm to individuals and groups, and it feels in the moment like the world is descending into chaos. This is why continual discussion about what free speech demands and why we choose to live by its dictates is absolutely vital.

Every university needs a just and efficient disciplinary system to handle behavioral violations when they do occur. This is important both for the integrity of the system for protecting people against harms and for the First Amendment and free speech itself. Free speech is hard enough to live with, and any failure to protect people when bad behavior happens outside that special arena will undoubtedly harm the underlying principle. Guidelines and limits are critical, but that does not mean enforcement will be simple in practice. More times than I can remember, I have been in situations where I had to make a very difficult judgment about how to enforce the rules limiting free speech. Imagine being in an auditorium where members of the audience begin to express their opposition to a speaker. Vocal disagreement (for example, boos); standing and turning one's back to the stage; holding signs and placards, perhaps bearing highly offensive words; chanting and shouting for a minute, or five minutes, or indefinitely—the question is what level of "disruption" you should be prepared to endure under the specific circumstances. This is difficult work.

After you have established an overall framework of robust free speech coupled with full and frequent explanations, recognized limits, and strong disciplinary measures, you must prepare to actually live successfully within this system. Which, to me, means you must figure out how you are going to ensure that the center continues to hold. In the society as a whole, you need strong institutions and a prepared citizenry to cope with a harsh environment. This must happen on a smaller scale of free speech on a university campus. People from all sides of the debate must speak out to condemn excesses, most especially by speakers who purport to represent their side of the debate, and you must have people ready to model how the debate should proceed. I do not mean that there should not be expressions of strong disagreement. But this should be able to happen in a manner that allows passionate disputes not to spill over into extremes.

Given that so many of the participants are so young, it is very likely that the debates will at times move to excess. Universities should be prepared for these moments, even if only by being aware of the likely problems and developing general plans for dealing with the circumstances of passionate controversies.

I am sorry to say that many universities in the past years have failed to prepare for excess and have failed in their reactions to excess. This is highly unfortunate for a reason few people fully grasp. For, of all the places in the society that should be able, visibly so, to exist successfully within the larger free speech regime created over the past century, it is universities. Universities should be the supreme model for how to understand, explain, and implement speech in public life. Universities are extremely important to the First Amendment, not least by showing how it should be followed. But universities, clearly, need to do a lot of work still in order to fulfill that responsibility and role.

I want to give another example of a major event that reveals the work to be done in building out the principle of academic freedom for universities. This was a case I was involved with; it happened while I was president of Columbia. It involved the visit and speech by the then president of Iran, Mahmoud Ahmadinejad. At the time, it was enormously controversial and created an extraordinary amount of national and international attention. Ahmadinejad was, to some, a menace to civil liberties in Iran and beyond, a threat to Israel (having said Iran would remove Israel "from the map"), and a denier of the Holocaust. To others, he was merely a crackpot dictator who was laughable on the international stage. He attended the annual meeting of the UN General Assembly in September of 2007. Under federal law he was subject to many travel restrictions, but he could legally move within a few miles of the United Nations. That radius included the campus of Columbia.

The dean and the faculty of the School of International and Public Affairs (SIPA) at Columbia invited Ahmadinejad to the campus to deliver an address. It is standard practice for such schools to invite heads of state to speak to faculty and students; indeed, it is expected as part of the academic mission that those within a university will listen to and debate world leaders. This includes not only "good" leaders but also "bad" ones. You want to know what people who hold power think and to engage with them. To most, Ahmadinejad certainly fit into the "bad" category.

Yet, some thought that Ahmadinejad fit into a different category, seeing him as so pernicious he should not be given a platform to speak at any university. That, however, was a matter for SIPA and its faculty to resolve, and they had chosen to engage rather than to ignore. It was a reasonable position. Given the importance to the world of Iran and its leaders, taking the measure of the person was important.

The speech became a mass media event, with stories and editorials in every major news outlet. Some people were supportive, and many others were irate. The campus was on high alert.

Given the extraordinarily high profile of the event and the important issues it raised for so many in our community,

I decided that we would have to take it out of an individual school and make it open to the university as part of a series we had called the World Leaders Forum. This was a program for inviting important figures and leaders to the campus to speak and then be subjected to questions primarily from students. We had hosted many such leaders, and the program had greater capacities to handle high-profile events.

In this case, I thought there was a serious risk that Ahmadinejad might agree in advance to take questions but then in the moment choose to leave before that could occur. Given the mounting criticisms of the university for providing a platform for him, that would be a disaster. To avoid this possibility, and to make sure that there was a strong critique of his words and behavior, we decided that it was necessary to have this critique happen at the beginning of the event and that the only person who should be asked to do this was me, in part because of my role as leader of the university and in part because the critique involved matters in which I had some expertise. Ahmadinejad's office was notified of the plan and offered the opportunity to withdraw. They decided to move forward, agreeing to our terms, including the specific issues I planned to raise in my remarks.

As we approached the day, the pressure against allowing Ahmadinejad to speak grew with ferocious intensity. I was contacted by countless people—public officials, donors, alumni—demanding that I withdraw the invitation. Often these demands were accompanied by threats of one sort or another, mostly involving withholding gifts and funding.

Yet the event went on and was viewed by millions. I gave the opening statement as planned. The speech followed. And people in the audience asked questions to which Ahmadinejad responded, though not always on point.

The controversy only seemed to grow in magnitude. Condemnation of Ahmadinejad was swift and severe, but there were many who countered that this was an example of what free speech in America is supposed to mean. Ahmadinejad's answers to questions became fodder for ridicule. At one point, in answering a question about the mistreatment of homosexuals in Iran, Ahmadinejad appeared to answer that there was no such problem because, in fact, there were no homosexuals in Iran. This led to a mocking cover of *The New Yorker* and a skit on *Saturday Night Live*.[23]

The criticism directed at me for allowing the event to go forward was, from my perspective at least, extreme. I faced significant personal threats and was put under special security for several weeks. Shortly after the event, I was in Paris on an official trip to meet with alumni. I was in a car when I received a call from Senator Arlen Specter of Pennsylvania. He proceeded to tell me that my remarks about the Iranian president had so infuriated the government of Iran that we were at risk of entering World War III. While that seemed preposterous, he nonetheless asked whether I could find some way publicly to apologize for my comments. I told him that was not possible. It is very hard to withstand the criticisms that say you are imposing immense costs on yourself and your institution by sticking to the silly idea of allowing this one speech. All the arguments that Holmes gave about why "persecution" of speakers is so "perfectly logical" apply with great force in the actual moment. The Ahmadinejad example is useful for two primary reasons. One is that it illustrates just how arduous it is in the moment of a major controversy about academic freedom to maintain course and hold on to principle. It was one of the most difficult experiences of my life. The second is that it reveals the principle of the freedom of the university is still in its infancy. This was borne out so clearly with the Ahmadinejad episode, because right after speaking at Columbia he went to do the same at the Council on Foreign Relations in midtown New York, and then on to meet with certain members of the press. The criticism directed at Columbia for hosting him was not repeated when he spoke at these other institutions. Somehow there was a widespread presumption that it was professionally appropriate for those places to confront and debate him but not for a leading university to do so. Americans should exhibit the same deference toward decisions of universities and recognize that universities have the same intellectual interest in confronting the world as it is.

THE UNIVERSITY IN THE PUBLIC REALM

One of the most vexing questions about the role of institutions like the press and universities is how they should interact with the public issues of their time. Journalism seeks to report on the events and issues, objectively and without a political agenda. It separates the "news" from the "editorial" function, where expressing opinions is the norm. Universities have chosen a somewhat different path. As we have seen, professors, by virtue of their commitment to the scholarly temperament, are expected to refrain from adopting a political agenda in the classroom or their scholarship. That does not preclude them from taking positions as a scholar on public issues, provided they abide by the spirit of the scholarly temperament. The university, as such, is often said to be "neutral" on political questions; an institutional position might "chill" faculty who might otherwise take a contrary position or might invite retaliation from external forces and injure the academic enterprise. Unlike the press, no university has set up a separate "editorial board" through which it would issue opinions on political and social questions and endorse or oppose candidates for public office.

When the press and universities are under attack, as they are today, the natural tendency is to try to retreat as a means of self-protection. The instinct is to withdraw and become less visible to the sources of hostility. That has been true today with some major press institutions—for instance, the decision of the *Washington Post* to end the practice of issuing political endorsements—and with many universities. This may or may not be a prudent reaction to improper political pressure, although my general reaction to such a strategy is quite negative. But the larger question is this: What role could be played by the university in society consistent with its broader mission? I believe universities have significant room in which to play a major social and political role and do so as a matter of course. To my mind, the university is a major political actor in the society, and embracing this role is a crucial piece of having a strong and confident identity, a robust sense of self.[24]

We might begin by recognizing a difference between taking positions on specific controversial issues (for example, no university has issued a declaration supporting a two-state solution to the Israel and Palestine conflict) and taking positions on the major questions of the era. I think one could make the case that even the former action is, in theory, within the bounds of the university's systemic role, just as the press does not lose its special standing because it adopts an "editorial" function, but that seems purely hypothetical at this point. It is the latter scenario that is most important, practically speaking, and something the university must be prepared to assert and defend as within its rights.

A parallel might be the role of the judiciary. The principle of the rule of law and the idea of a judicial temperament command judges not to become political actors when performing their judicial functions. Yet, for a variety of reasons, most significantly because all law necessarily has an open-ended character that has to be filled in order for law to work, judges must turn to some understandings of the political culture in which law is made. This is true no matter how originalist or textualist you claim to be. In the end, judges have to find some line, however vague or difficult to articulate, between a political viewpoint and sensitivity to a large political climate to be grasped and applied. So it is with universities.

For universities, we can look again at the area of affirmative action (and diversity, equity, and inclusion) as a case in point.

As suggested above, I have supported affirmative action in universities and been involved in the constitutional debates and decisions surrounding it, both in some of the principal cases and through my writings and speeches. I think affirmative action has made immense contributions to scholarship and education of all students, but just as importantly it has helped society get closer to racial justice.

Affirmative action began in the early 1970s, and every selective university across the country embraced the policy. Since *Brown v. Board of Education* (1954), the quest to deal with the severe injustices of slavery and Jim Crow laws and so-called de facto discrimination had preoccupied many Americans. There was broad recognition across all sectors of society that invidious discrimination had to end, and the centuries of oppression needed to be redressed. Hence affirmative action in universities, whose student bodies were almost entirely male and white. But change came to every other institution in America, from business to media to organizations of every kind, public and private. Of course, there was opposition, and that would ebb and flow over the ensuing decades. But the nation had been set on a new course.

The history of constitutional cases dealing with these policies and practices can be quickly summarized: In *Regents of the University of California v. Bakke* (1978), the Court split 4–4 on a case involving quotas for African Americans at the UC Davis medical school. Justice Lewis F. Powell, Jr., was the swing vote, and his opinion became the guide for universities on affirmative action, even though what he said was not the official holding of the Court. He drew a distinction between affirmative action intended to remedy past societal discrimination, which would not be permitted under the Fourteenth Amendment, and affirmative action that was done because of the "educational benefits" of a "diverse" student body. Although the distinction was not entirely clear, it stood as the benchmark until the Supreme Court agreed with him in 2003 in *Grutter v. Bollinger*, when a clear majority of the Court affirmed the policy as consistent with the Equal Protection Clause of the Fourteenth Amendment. Only a few years ago, in 2023, *Grutter v. Bollinger* was effectively overturned by a new Court majority in the case of *Students for Fair Admissions v. President and Fellows of Harvard College*. In the opinion for the majority, Chief Justice Roberts emphasized that it was time to close this exception to the constitutional proscription against the use of race in decision-making. He further asserted that the universities had not provided sufficient evidence of educational benefits to overcome the deference properly afforded universities under the Constitution.[25]

It is my view, which I have articulated many times over the decades, that affirmative action in universities made a significant contribution to the advancement of Blacks, Hispanics, and Native Americans (the primary groups typically included in these policies), and *SFFA* will be a tragedy for the nation, given the lost opportunities to achieve the dream of *Brown v. Board of Education*. At this point, we still do not know the full reach of the *SFFA* decision, but we do know it is not the end of the revanchism. The Trump administration has made it a central mission to eliminate so-called DEI policies and practices; the full strength of the government is being bent to that purpose. My concern here, however, is not so much that backlash and the grave harm it will cause. I want to highlight a separate question: Over the period of approximately a half century, was it wrong in principle for universities to embrace these policies because they involved judgments about what was best for the society? Until *Bakke*, and perhaps even after (since Powell's opinion was only dictum, meaning it is not dispositive of the holding in the case and therefore is not binding law), universities adopted affirmative action policies on the rationale of a much-needed remedy for past and present discrimination. That was consistent with the broad majority sentiment of the era. Even after Powell in *Bakke*, universities saw the need for students to learn across the divides of race and ethnicity and to produce better citizens. That, too, is a substantive judgment about what the nation needs. Is this wrong?

I believe this was (and is) both entirely appropriate for universities to do and well within their autonomy under the principle of the freedom of the university. Far more than we commonly realize, universities are built on judgments about what serves the national and public interest, and that is, generally speaking, a good thing. What subjects to research, to teach and in what ways, what values of character and intellect to nurture, what combination of students with different backgrounds and talents with what educational experiences will produce the best citizens—these and so many other decisions are inherently connected to ideas about the world we want to live in.

Again, it is true that universities, generally, refrain from taking positions on many specific political questions. A well-known statement at the University of Chicago issued during the era of the Vietnam War and the intense opposition on university campuses made a strong case for universities not to take institutional positions on controversial public issues. This makes sense, as far as it goes. No university I know has issued a declaration about its views on issues of tax policy (except as it is applied to universities!) or about the need to reform the Electoral College or, to put a fine point on it, about who should be elected as president in the next election. I think that's generally wise. But I also do not believe it would be unacceptable with or entirely inconsistent with the principle of freedom of the university. I can imagine a different world in which the balance of interests at stake might be struck differently. In any case, the question of the roles the university can and should play is a much more complex one than the question of what statements on public issues should university officials refrain from issuing.[26]

We should also bear in mind the analogy of the press and the principle of freedom of the press. No one has ever suggested that only the "news" side of the paper should be protected, or that the "editorial" side taking political positions negates the reasons for the protections. We assume this is part of what being the press is. We welcome the opinions as such, especially given that we say we are committed to a public debate that is rich and robust with opinions of all kinds from all quarters.

The same should be true for universities. There are, of course, other considerations to take into account. The idea that a university opinion chills debate within the university has a reality to it. But I have to say that in general, I have found that not to be a serious risk. Faculty are hardly reticent about expressing their own views, and, indeed, often become more vocal when the institution has set down an opinion. Nevertheless, it is certainly a factor to be kept in mind, along with the interest in having as many viewpoints on difficult issues as we can get.

The other concern is the risk of retaliation. The current political reality is proof of the seriousness of this risk. But the risk of not taking any position is a graver one, in my view.

Every single day, universities make judgments in accord with scholarly standards and the scholarly temperament about what the nation and the world needs. And these judgments happen in an ever-ongoing conversation with the broader society and world. We should embrace and acknowledge this role. The issue is when a university has stopped being a university (in the sense we have described it) and become a partisan political organization. We know the difference when we see it, even though there may be instances when the line is difficult to point to. But it is a line we must learn to live with and be honest about.

THE FUTURE

Assuming this troubled era passes, and universities are not so severely hobbled by government attacks, and assuming American democracy survives, the modern university has a brilliant future. The greatest joy of being a university president is to gaze across the whole institution, and the university system broadly, and to witness the amazing discoveries that are being made and the potential for further investigation. I have noted above that the history of the modern American university is one marked by significant growth—in the areas of knowledge to be explored, in the students to be educated, and in the interactions with the world. The physical expansion that undergirds this ever-enlarging mission is a marker of this flourishing reality. In the next era of the university, my deepest hope is that the university as I have sketched it here will be appreciated, fortified with constitutional and other protections, filled with confidence about its singular role in society, and modest about its peculiar structure and place in a good life.

Every university, and certainly all of them together, are like a gigantic storehouse of ideas and intellectual capacity waiting to be deployed. Many faculty on their own figure out how to take scholarship into the public realm and use it for the common good. In my early years as a professor, I saw this in its finest form. An older colleague was the leading scholar in his fields and had a general intellectual capacity that made him brilliant in every conversation about any subject. He was also gifted at practical affairs. He helped draft major legislation, he was consulted regularly by political and corporate figures, and he could contribute to finding solutions to any problem. These unique capabilities made him all the more admired. As another colleague said of him: It was as if all of us were on a train while he was flying in an airplane. The interaction of the scholarly and practical worlds combined in him to make him extraordinary and special. But he did this all on his own. What if the university made it part of its mission to provide the help necessary for all faculty who want to be this way but could not easily do so themselves? That would seem like a new dimension of the university.

To listen inside any university is to hear this idea promoted daily. It is a routine claim of schools and programs to declare that they wish to combine theory and practice, to bring research to action, to use research to solve the world's most pressing problems, and so on. And, if you look, you will find many examples of this happening. But there is little effort by universities to become organized and systematic in fulfilling this larger mission of engaging with the world beyond the academic gates.

There are two very notable exceptions. The first, and by far the most important, is in academic medicine. All research universities have fundamental research programs in the life and biological sciences, as well as other areas of science with sometimes direct relevance to medicine (for example, chemistry, physics, engineering, and computer science). And many have health clinics and hospitals that deliver care to the general public (sometimes the university owns the hospital and sometimes it has an affiliation agreement with a separately owned hospital, but the result is the same for our purposes here). This is a perfect example of how a university can do both basic research and very practical things, using and exchanging the knowledge from one to the other.

The other concrete example of an organized effort to combine research and practical action is with the so-called technology transfer offices of universities. Beginning in the 1980s, the U.S. government decided to allow, indeed to encourage, universities to keep whatever revenues they achieved by licensing research for commercial purposes. This set universities on a path to establish offices in the central administration that would help facilitate this transfer of research into commercial applications. Over the decades, these offices have grown considerably and are by now well-established programs, which help bring faculty together with outside companies to develop products arising out of the research discoveries. There have been many spectacularly successful cases, with enormous financial rewards for the universities and the researchers, as well as benefits to the public.[27]

If we are serious about this dimension of the university—and I strongly believe we should be—we must develop university institutions that can combine academic research and capacities with external parties to make things better for the world. Occasionally, academics are naturally good at engaging with public problems and issues, but generally speaking we are not. The desire to accomplish practical things by using academic capabilities is far more universal than the ability to fulfill the desire. Yet, with assistance and imagination, great things can be accomplished. A group of us at Columbia undertook to create such a university-wide structure to enable these kinds of interactions between academics and the outside world involving practical problem-solving and general human fulfillment. In the course of that, we studied what was happening at other universities and found dozens initiating similar projects. It does seem to be a very favorable trend among higher education institutions. And the possibilities for productive collaborations around real human issues seem infinite.

It turns out that solving practical problems is just about as hard as discovering new knowledge through scholarship, so one needs to approach this new university mission with a sober willingness to do the hard work that will most certainly be called for. And like anything of this magnitude, you will need to take the time required to determine what's involved and where this might go for each institution. But, based on my own experience with moving things in a more practical or human realm, this is a scenario where success will build on success.

I raise these possibilities in order to show how wide the potential horizon is for the university to serve the society and the world. The core of its activities will remain in place, I am confident. That doesn't mean fields will not change or that some new ones will emerge. The very best faculty and departments are always looking ahead to where the search for knowledge should take us. But there are also very significant opportunities for expanding the core role. Of all the failings and shortcomings of the contemporary university, the one that strikes me as the most valid is that we are too isolated from the world around us, too prone to arcane and inaccessible language, and too limited in our capacities to reach out to the general public with expertise and humility. Taking on these new dimensions I have described might serve us well in reducing those frictions. But it would also bring great benefits to the university and its central mission of seeking knowledge. To return to where we began, and Montaigne's insight: "There is no desire more natural than the desire for knowledge. We try all the ways that can lead us to it. When reason fails us, we use experience." Adding experience to reason would make the university all the stronger.[28]

CONCLUSION

UNIVERSITIES ARE PLACES WHERE YOU CAN SPEND your life. Most faculty do. That, in itself, says a lot about the meaning one can find in this role. The appeal of laboring, largely by yourself but often in the company of colleagues, for knowledge is significant, and the work is sustaining. In a world in which mobility and changing careers are increasingly the norm, there is something distinctive about the academy.

We have seen how the university has come to be composed, its structure, its ways of operating, and its culture. All of it is odd, in the sense that this defies normal understandings about how people behave in organizational settings, about what motivates them, and about the sources of satisfaction in life. And then, we have seen how the First Amendment has evolved over the past century, during roughly the same period of time that the university became what it is today. There, too, we found something unique, counterintuitive, and out of the ordinary compared with how other nations have responded to and answered these fundamental questions. These have become two intimately related institutions, joined together in a common mission and with shared premises regarding how to think about human nature and the ends of life, and they now make up the center of American life. They demonstrate how complex social life can be, and how we can navigate our way through it.

The modern university and the First Amendment share an intellectual spirit rooted in the Enlightenment values embraced by America's Founders. That spirit is something we should never take for granted. It is very ambitious and certainly high minded. In the nitty gritty of daily life, especially daily political life, this can all seem naïve and idealistic to a fault. But you won't be able to convince the people who have spent their lives in the university, nor the country's judges and justices, from the Right and the Left, that all this is just fluff in a world of hard power. To them these institutions are noble, commendable, and represent the best way to live.

But why should the rest of America care?

The normal response would be to say that the university has brought you a bounty of benefits, from your health to your smartphone. Yet, as true as that argument is, to my mind it misses the heart of the matter.

We all want to know, to learn, and to have knowledge. This is as basic to each of us as Montaigne said. In my family, neither of my parents attended college; my mother, in fact, did not complete high school. Their lives were interrupted by World War II. Growing up I watched them always finding ways to learn and to teach themselves. (My father, feeling the need to learn about public speaking, took a Dale Carnegie course to that end.) They always respected the university and never felt resentment. To them it was a continuous line from what they could know through to the knowledge of the highest experts. So I think it is for just about all of us, and society is far richer and better off if that desire is given opportunity to thrive.

There are endless reasons why we might want to know more about something. Maybe we want to build a boat, or make more money, or find the best university for our child. As humans we constantly want to know more, no matter what our position in life. And that, in itself, is a source of profound satisfaction. We want the capacity to know, a complex and challenging skill to master, and we want to exercise that capacity, and we want that because that is what it means to be human. To think, to reason, to consider, to reflect, and then to decide and to act—these are the things every single one of us wants to be able to do, and to do even better than we are currently able to.

The designs of the First Amendment and the university are reflective of that desire and serve, together, as a formal structure that advances it. This is a special feature of the American system. In many societies, the basic human desire to know is viewed as something to be suppressed, even a threat. You are allowed to know only what is given, expected to profess those sanctioned beliefs, to be obedient and otherwise silent.

With our Constitution and our institutions, the opposite is true in the United States. And one needs only look around oneself to see the better life this yields.

The university is the *institutional* manifestation of this

common desire. All it knows is public. Its knowledge is our knowledge. It is true that no single one of us will ever know but the slightest fraction of the whole. And as knowledge expands that will be ever more true. As a university president, I felt more and more ignorant the more I looked across the institution and saw what was known. Once I asked a Nobel Prize physicist whether, if I really worked at it, I could ever hope to understand quantum mechanics. He thought for a minute and then said, emphatically, "No, it's not possible." Be that as it may, it is nevertheless true that my incapacity to understand what is known does not lessen my respect and gratitude for that knowledge or for those who possess it. But we all feel this in our lives. Individually we know so little; but collectively we know a lot. That is, perhaps, a definition of the university, and of America itself.

ACKNOWLEDGMENTS

FOR A BOOK THAT BRINGS TOGETHER THOUGHTS AND experiences over many years, it is impossible to recognize and thank all the people who have helped along the way. I wish it were otherwise, not least because the help was so great. For this specific book, the ideas began to form in the course of writing and delivering two recent lectures.

The first was the Professor Ronna Greff Schneider Constitutional Issues in Educational Law Lecture I delivered at the University of Cincinnati College of Law in February of 2025. That was followed in April with the Sidney N. Zubrow Memorial Lecture at the Columbia Institute for Ideas and Imagination at the Columbia Global Center in Paris. These venues allowed me the opportunity to interact with audiences and colleagues in that critical process of figuring out the right framework and substance for what I wanted to say. Several people were extremely important in this stage; among them were Richard Axel, Carol Becker, Vincent Blasi, Simon Glendinning, and Nicolas Lemann.

Following a press interview in the weeks after these lectures, I was contacted by Dan Gerstle, editor in chief at W. W. Norton, about the possibility of writing this book. That conversation provided the spark for launching this undertaking and bringing it to fruition. All along the way, Dan was the ideal guide and editor, leaving me with the conviction that this would not have come about were it not for him.

Many other friends and colleagues have contributed enormously to what I offer in this book. I especially thank Floyd Abrams, Amy Gutmann, Jameel Jaffer, Ira Katznelson, Liz Magill, Mark Mazower (who, as Director of the Columbia Institute for Ideas and Imagination, also orchestrated the Zubrow Lecture), Robert Post, Gerald Rosberg, David Stone, Geoffrey Stone, and Cornelia Woll. My wife, Jean, as always, played a vital role at every stage, not least in giving meaning to the whole enterprise. And, finally, I am very grateful to my assistants who have shepherded this process from draft to draft to final manuscript and to publication. Britt Hefelfinger, associate director of strategic projects at Columbia, was outstanding; as were the contributions of the research assistants, Peter Camardo, Saul Roselaar, and Yunxuan Wendy Wu.

NOTES

INTRODUCTION

1. *HHS, ED, and GSA Announce Additional Measures to End Anti-Semitic Harassment on College Campuses*, U.S. GENERAL SERVICES ADMINISTRATION (Mar. 3, 2025); Michael C. Bender & Sheryl Gay Stolberg, *Trump Administration Freezes $1 Billion for Cornell and $790 Million for Northwestern, Officials Say*, N.Y. TIMES (Apr. 8, 2025); *Joint Task Force to Combat Anti-Semitism Statement Regarding Harvard University*, U.S. DEPARTMENT OF EDUCATION (Apr. 14, 2025); *U.S. Department of Education's Office for Civil Rights Finds the University of Pennsylvania Has Violated Title IX*, U.S. DEPARTMENT OF EDUCATION (Apr. 28, 2025); Letter from Josh Gruenbaum, Comm'r of the Fed. Acquisition Serv., General Services Administration, Sean R. Keveney, Acting General Counsel, U.S. Dep't Health & Human Servs. & Thomas E. Wheeler, Acting General Counsel, U.S. Dep't. of Education, to Dr. Alan M. Garber, President, Harvard University & Penny Pritzker, Lead Member, Harvard Corporation (Apr. 11, 2025); Letter from Josh Gruenbaum, Comm'r of the Fed. Acquisition Serv., General Services Administration, Sean R. Keveney, Acting General Counsel, U.S. Dep't Health & Human Servs. & Thomas E. Wheeler, Acting General Counsel, U.S. Dep't. of Education, to Dr. Katrina Armstrong, Interim President, Columbia University, David Greenwald Co-Chair, Columbia Board of Trustees, & Claire Shipman, Co-Chair, Columbia Board of Trustees (Mar. 13, 2025).

2. Sharon Otterman, *Columbia Agrees to $200 Million Fine to Settle Fight with Trump*, N.Y. TIMES (July 23, 2025); Alan M. Garber, *Uphold-*

ing Our Values, Defending Our University, HARVARD OFFICE OF THE PRESIDENT (Apr. 21, 2025).

3. Michael C. Bender, *Trump Pushes to Restrict Harvard's International Students from Entering U.S.*, N.Y. TIMES (June 4, 2025); Sharon Otterman, *Trump Escalates Attack on Columbia by Threatening Its Accreditation*, N.Y. TIMES (June 4, 2025).

4. American Ass'n of University Professors, Report of a Special Committee: Political Interference and Academic Freedom in Florida's Public Higher Education System (2023); Jennifer Ruth, *Subnational Authoritarianism and the Campaign to Control Higher Education*, ACADEME MAGAZINE, Fall 2023, at 10.

5. Memorandum on Suspension of Security Clearances and Evaluation of Government Contracts, 2025 DAILY COMP. PRES. DOC. 103 (Feb. 25, 2025); Exec. Order No. 14230, 90 Fed. Reg. 11781 (Mar. 11, 2025) (Addressing Risks from Perkins Coie LLP); Exec. Order No. 14237, 90 Fed. Reg. 13039 (Mar. 20, 2025) (Addressing Risks from Paul Weiss); Exec. Order No. 14246, 90 Fed. Reg. 13997 (Mar. 28, 2025) (Addressing Risks from Jenner & Block); Exec. Order No. 14250, 90 Fed. Reg. 14549 (Apr. 3, 2025) (Addressing Risks from WilmerHale); Exec. Order No. 14263, 90 Fed. Reg. 15615 (Apr. 15, 2025) (Addressing Risks from Susman Godfrey); Tobi Raji, *Trump Picks One-Judge Texas Court for Lawsuit over CBS Harris Interview*, WASHINGTON POST (Oct. 31, 2024); Michael M. Grynbaum and Jim Rutenberg, *Trump Sues ABC and Stephanopoulos Saying They Defamed Him*, N.Y. TIMES (Mar. 18, 2024); Alanna Durkin Richer, Larry Neumeister & Jill Colvin, *Trump Sues Wall Street Journal and Media Mogul Rupert Murdoch over Reporting on Epstein Ties*, ASSOCIATED PRESS (July 16, 2025); Liam Reilly, *Trump Baselessly Accuses News Media of 'Illegal' Behavior and Corruption in DOJ Speech*, CNN (Mar. 14, 2025); Clara Harter, *FCC Investigating San Francisco Radio Station That Shared Location of Undercover ICE Agents*, L.A. TIMES (Feb. 6, 2025).

6. Kevin Carey, *What Colleges Should Learn from Newspapers' Decline*, CHRONICLE OF HIGHER EDUCATION (Apr. 3, 2009).

7. *See* SOL GITTLEMAN, AN ACCIDENTAL TRIUMPH: THE IMPROBABLE HISTORY OF AMERICAN HIGHER EDUCATION (2023).

8. MICHEL DE MONTAIGNE, *Of Experience,* in THE COMPLETE ESSAYS OF MONTAIGNE, 815 (Donald M. Frame trans., Stanford Univ. Press 1958) (1588).

CHAPTER ONE: THE UNIVERSITY

1. SAMUEL JOHNSON, ROGER LONSDALE & JOHN MULLAN, THE LIVES OF THE POETS: A SELECTION (2009).

2. Lee C. Bollinger, *Announcing the Columbia Climate School,* COLUMBIA OFFICE OF THE PRESIDENT: ANNOUNCEMENTS (July 10, 2020).

3. MURRAY L. WEIDENBAUM, THE EVOLVING CORPORATE BOARD (May 1, 1994).

4. *Table 105.50. Number of Educational Institutions, by Level and Control of Institution: Academic Years 2010–11 through 2020–21,* NATIONAL CENTER FOR EDUCATION STATISTICS: DIGEST OF EDUCATIONAL STATISTICS (Sept. 2022); *Our Members,* ASSOCIATION OF AMERICAN UNIVERSITIES (AAU) (last visited July 30, 2025).

5. Naomi Grimley, *Identity 2016: 'Global Citizenship' Rising, Poll Suggests,* BBC (Apr. 28, 2016).

CHAPTER TWO: THE FIRST AMENDMENT

1. *Schenck v. United States,* 249 U.S. 47 (1919); *See* Geoffrey R. Stone, *Reflections on the First Amendment: The Evolution of the American Jurisprudence of Free Expression,* 141 PROCS. AM. PHIL. SOC'Y 251 (1987); *See* FREDERICK SCHAUER, *The Exceptional First Amendment, in* AMERICAN EXCEPTIONALISM AND HUMAN RIGHTS 29 (Michael Ignatieff ed., 2005) [hereinafter Schauer, *Exceptional First Amendment*] ("In numerous dimensions, the American approach is exceptional . . .").

2. *See* Robert C. Post, *Community and the First Amendment,* 29 ARIZ. ST. L.J. 473, 481–84 (1997) (explaining that the First Amendment creates a cultural place for democratic dialogue, and that "the relationship between freedom of speech and community is thus highly dependent upon contingent matters of history and culture").

3. *See, e.g.,* Marco Rubio, *Protecting and Championing Free Speech at the State Department,* U.S. DEP'T OF STATE (Apr. 16, 2025) (describing the closure of the Counter Foreign Information Manipulation and Interference [R/FIMI] office as an effort to "preserve and protect the freedom for Americans to exercise their free speech"); Robert Winterton, *America Must Fight for Free Speech in 2025,* NETCHOICE (Jan. 13, 2025) (describing the regulation of online platforms as a First Amendment and free speech issue); David J. Bier, *US Citizens Don't Have First Amendment Rights If Noncitizens Don't,* CATO INSTITUTE (Apr. 15, 2025) (criticizing the Trump administration's revocation of green cards and visas on the basis of "beliefs, statements, or associations" as an "attack to free speech" and a "government intervention in society"); *See* SCHAUER, *Exceptional First Amendment, supra* note 1; Anu Bradford & Eric A. Posner, *Universal Exceptionalism in International Law,* 52 HARV. INT'L L.J. 1 (2011) ("European human rights norms do not prohibit the suppression of parties and certain types of derogatory speech protected by the First Amendment to the U.S. Constitution.").

4. U.S. CONST. amend. I; AKIL REED AMAR, THE BILL OF RIGHTS: CREATION AND RECONSTRUCTION 3 (1998) ("The 1789 Bill of Rights was, unsurprisingly, a creature of its time."); *See, e.g.,* Alexander Meiklejohn, *What Does the First Amendment Mean?,* 20 U. CHI. L. REV. 461 (1953); William J. Brennan, Jr., *The Supreme Court and the Meiklejohn Interpretation of the First Amendment,* 79 HARV. L. REV. 1 (1965); Lee C. Bollinger, *The Future and the First Amendment,* 18 CAP. U.L. REV. 221 (1989); Erwin Chemerinsky, *History, Tradition, the Supreme Court, and the First Amendment,* 44 HASTINGS L.J. 901 (1990); David M. Rabban, *The Emergence of the First Amendment Doctrine,* 50 U. CHI. L. REV. 1205 (1983); Frederick Schauer, *The Role of the People in First Amendment Theory,* 74 CALIF. L. REV. 761, 784 (1986) ("First amendment doctrine is now enormously complex, consisting of the selective application of a large number of different principles, standards, and rules not capable of easy or mechanical application."); *See generally* Adam Griffin, Note, *First Amendment Originalism: The Original Law and a Theory of Legal Change as Applied to the Freedom of Speech and of the Press,* 17 FIRST

AMEND. L. REV. 91 (2018); *See* Jud Campbell, *Natural Rights and the First Amendment*, 127 YALE L.J. 246, 249–50 (2017) (examining judicial and scholarly debates of the past century and concluding that some scholars find "the meanings of speech and press freedoms at the Founding remain remarkably hazy"); *But see Id.* at 251–57 (arguing that shared, nuanced understandings of speech and press freedom existed alongside with disagreement about their application during the Founding Era).

5. *See* David Yassky, *Eras of the First Amendment*, 91 COLUM. L. REV. 1699, 1700, 1710–13 (1991) (explaining that one version of the Founding history of the First Amendment emphasizes the effect of the Enlightenment and commitment to tolerance, and arguing that the First Amendment was a "bulwark against centralization" during the discussion of the Sedition Act and the colonial debate over abolition literature); Leonard W. Levy, *Liberty and the First Amendment: 1790–1800*, 68 AM. HIST. REV. 22 (1962) (examining the history of press regulations and the passage of the First Amendment at the founding).

6. *Schenck v. United States*, 249 U.S. 47 (1919); *Frohwerk v. United States*, 249 U.S. 204 (1919); *Debs v. United States*, 249 U.S. 211 (1919).

7. Espionage Act of 1917, Pub. L. No. 65–24, 40 Stat. 217, 219.

8. *Schenck*, 249 U.S. at 49 ("[T]he defendant willfully conspired to have printed and circulated to men who had been called and accepted for military service under the Act of May 18, 1917, a document set forth and alleged to be calculated to cause such insubordination and obstruction."); *Frohwerk*, 240 U.S. at 205 ("[The defendant was] engaged in the preparation and publication of a newspaper, the Missouri Staats Zeitung, to violate the Espionage Act . . .[,] to cause disloyalty, mutiny, and refusal of duty in the military and naval forces of the United States by the same publications . . ."); Thomas Doherty, *Eugene Debs: When a Prisoner Ran for President*, BRANDEIS NOW (Apr. 21, 2023) ("In the election of 1920, Eugene V. Debs, the Socialist Party presidential candidate, polled nearly a million votes without ever hitting the campaign trail.").

9. *Debs*, 249 U.S. at 216 ("Without going into further particulars, we

are of opinion that the verdict on the fourth count, for obstructing and attempting to obstruct the recruiting service of the United States, must be sustained."); *Frohwerk*, 249 U.S. at 210 ("Upon the whole case, we are driven to the conclusion that the record shows no ground upon which the judgment can be reversed."); *Schenck*, 249 U.S. at 53 (affirming the conviction).

10. Catharine Pierce Wells, *Oliver Wendell Holmes, Jr., and the American Civil War*, 40 J. SUP. CT. HIST. 282, 282 ("Oliver Wendell Holmes, Jr. spent three terrible years fighting in the Civil War. . . . He was wounded three times, suffered a nearly fatal bout of dysentery, and endured the deaths of many of his closest friends."); Lee C. Bollinger, *The Open-Minded Soldier and the University*, 32 MICH. Q. REV. at 1, 17 (1993) ("[Holmes] almost lusted after self-doubt, because he was repelled by the behavior of true believers [among whom, significantly, he counted himself when he served as a soldier in the Civil War].").

11. *Schenck*, 249 U.S. at 51, 52 ("Words which, ordinarily and in many places, would be within the freedom of speech protected by the First Amendment may become subject to prohibition when of such a nature and used in such circumstances as to create a clear and present danger that they will bring about the substantive evils which Congress has a right to prevent.").

12. *Frohwerk v. United States*, 249 U.S. 204, 209 (1919) ("But we must take the case on the record as it is, and, on that record, it is impossible to say that it might not have been found that the circulation of the paper was in quarters where a little breath would be enough to kindle a flame, and that the fact was known and relied upon by those who sent the paper out.").

13. *Debs v. United States*, 249 U.S. 211, 216 (1919).

14. 250 U.S. 616, 616–17, 621–22 (1919) ("Even if their primary purpose and intent was to aid the cause of the Russian Revolution, the plan of action which they adopted necessarily involved, before it could be realized, defeat of the war program of the United States."); Sedition Act of 1918, Pub. L. No. 65–150, 40 Stat. 553, 553.

15. *Id.* at 630 (Holmes, J., dissenting).
16. *Id.*
17. JOHN MILTON, AREOPAGITICA (1644); JOHN STUART MILL, ON LIB-ERTY (1859); LEE C. BOLLINGER, THE TOLERANT SOCIETY: FREE SPEECH AND EXTREMIST SPEECH IN AMERICA (1986); LEE C. BOL-LINGER, IN SEARCH OF AN OPEN MIND: SPEECHES AND WRITINGS (2024).
18. *Abrams,* 250 U.S. at 631.
19. *See* MICHAEL HUEMER, *Can Constitutions Limit Government?, in* THE OXFORD HANDBOOK OF FREEDOM (David Schmidtz & Carmen E. Pavel eds., 2018), at 350.
20. 274 U.S. 357 (1927); *Id.* at 376 (Brandeis, J., concurring).
21. *Near v. Minnesota,* 283 U.S. 697 (1931); *Cantwell v. Connecticut,* 310 U.S. 296 (1940).
22. LANDON R. Y. STORRS, *McCarthyism and the Second Red Scare, in* OXFORD RESEARCH ENCYCLOPEDIA OF AMERICAN HISTORY (July 2, 2015) ("Defining the American Communist Party as a serious threat to national security, government and nongovernment actors at national, state, and local levels developed a range of mechanisms for identifying and punishing Communists and their alleged sympathizers."); 341 U.S. 494 (1951).
23. Michal R. Belknap, *Why* Dennis v. United States *is a Landmark Case,* 34 J. SUP. CT. HIST. 289, 294 (2009) ("Nothing better illustrates America's lack of commitment during the McCarthy era than does *Dennis v. United States* and the legal war on the Communist party that it unleashed."); 341 U.S. at 509–10.
24. *See, e.g.,* Vincent Blasi, *The Pathological Perspective and the First Amendment,* 85 COLUM. L. REV. 449, 450 (1985) ("[C]ertain segments of time are of special significance for the preservation of the basic liberties of expression and inquiry because the most serious threats to those liberties tend to be concentrated in abnormal periods. To define such periods with any degree of precision is a challenge that must await an examination of the reasons why courts ought to adopt the pathological perspective.").

25. 395 U.S. 444 (1969).
26. 432 U.S. 43 (1977); 562 U.S. 443 (2011).
27. *Hague v. Comm. for Indus. Org.*, 307 U.S. 496 (1939) ("[S]treets and parks . . . have immemorially been held in trust for the use of the public and, time out of mind, have been used for purposes of assembly, communicating thoughts between citizens, and discussing public questions."); *Near v. Minnesota,* 283 U.S. 697 (1931) (striking down a Minnesota "gag law" that suppressed a newspaper for publishing "malicious, scandalous, and defamatory" content and holding that prior restraints are presumptively unconstitutional); *See Cantwell v. Connecticut,* 310 U.S. 296 (1940); *Lovell v. City of Griffin,* 303 U.S. 404 (1938); *Schneider v. Town of Irvington,* 308 U.S. 147, 161, 162 (1939) (invalidating municipal bans on hand-to-hand leaflet distribution in public streets, even where the city argued litter control justified restrictions); *Martin v. City of Struthers,* 319 U.S. 141 (1943) (striking down a ban on door-to-door distribution of handbills, arguing that door-to-door advocacy is protected speech).
28. 376 U.S. 254 (1964).
29. *Curtis Publishing Co. v. Butts,* 388 U.S. 130 (1967); 376 U.S. at 270.
30. 376 U.S. at 274; *Id.* at 300–01 (Goldberg, J., concurring) ("The opinion of the Court conclusively demonstrates the chilling effect of the Alabama libel laws on First Amendment freedoms in the area of race relations.").
31. Alexander Meiklejohn, Free Speech and Its Relation to Self-Government 69–70 (1948) ("And it is that authority of these truth-seeking activities which the First Amendment recognizes as uniquely significant when it says that the freedom of public discussion shall never be abridged. It is the failure to recognize the uniqueness of that authority which has led the Supreme Court to break down the difference between the First Amendment and the Fifth.").
32. *See, e.g.,* Anthony Lewis, New York Times v. Sullivan *Reconsidered: Time to Return to the Central Meaning of the First Amendment,* 83 Colum. L. Rev. 603 (1983); Kermit Hall, Keynote Address, New York Times v. Sullivan: *The Case and Its Times,* 1 Drake L. Rev. 21 (1990);

David A. Anderson, *The Promises of* New York Times v. Sullivan, 20 Roger Williams U.L. REV. 1, 16–17 (2015); Ronald D. Rotunda, *The Confirmation Process for Supreme Court Justices in the Modern Era*, 37 EMORY L.J. 559, 573–74 (1988) (detailing attacks on Bork's candidacy on the basis of his First Amendment–related academic writings); ALEXANDER MEIKLEJOHN, FREE SPEECH AND ITS RELATION TO SELF-GOVERNMENT 25–26 (1948) ("What is essential is not that everyone shall speak, but that everything worth saying shall be said.").

33. 403 U.S. 15 (1971).

34. *Id.* at 16, 19 n.3, 21, 23, 25.

35. *Tinker v. Des Moines Indep. Cmty. Sch. Dist.*, 393 U.S. 503, 504, 506 (1969).

36. *R.A.V. v. City of St. Paul*, 505 U.S. 377 (1992). *Virginia v. Black*, 538 U.S. 343 (2003).

37. *Abrams v. United States*, 250 U.S. 616, 630 (1919) (Holmes, J., dissenting).

38. *Abrams*, 250 U.S. at 629 (Holmes, J., dissenting).

39. *See, e.g.*, PAUL STARR, THE CREATION OF THE MEDIA: POLITICAL ORIGINS OF MODERN COMMUNICATIONS (2004); W. Joseph Campbell, *Yellow Journalism*, in INT'L ENCYC. J. STUD. (Tim P. Vos & Folker Hanusch eds., 2019).

40. Lee C. Bollinger, *2018 Tanner Lectures, Part 1*, Off. of the President; DOUGLASS CATER, THE FOURTH BRANCH OF GOVERNMENT (1959); HERBERT BRUCKER, FREEDOM OF INFORMATION (1949).

41. *New York Times Co. v. United States*, 403 U.S. 713 (1971) [hereinafter *Pentagon Papers*].

42. *New York Times Co. v. United States*, 403 U.S. 713 (1971).

43. ALEXANDER M. BICKEL, THE MORALITY OF CONSENT 80 (1975).

44. Potter Stewart, *"Or of the Press,"* 26 U. CAL. L. S.F. L.J. 631 (1975) ("the Free Press Clause extends protection to an institution. The publishing business is, in short, the only organized private business that is given explicit constitutional protection.").

45. 408 U.S. 665, 667–79, 684 (1972); *Id.* at 710 (Powell, J., concurring) ("The balance of these vital constitutional and societal interests on a

case-by-case basis accords with the tried and traditional way of adjudicating such questions."); *E.g., Pell v. Procunier*, 417 U.S. 817 (1974) (denying reporters special access right to California prisons to conduct face-to-face interviews).

46. Communications Act of 1934, 47 U.S.C. §§ 151–622 (2018); *See* Fairness Doctrine, 47 C.F.R. § 73.1910 (later repealed); *see also* Act of September 14, 1959, s 1, 73 Stat. 557, amending 47 U.S.C. s 315(a) (affirming FCC's fairness doctrine).

47. *Red Lion Broadcasting Co. v. FCC*, 395 U.S. 367, 389 (1969). ("There is nothing in the First Amendment which prevents the Government from requiring a licensee to share his frequency with others and to conduct himself as a proxy or fiduciary with obligations to present those views and voices which are representative of his community and which would otherwise, by necessity, be barred from the airwaves.").

48. 418 U.S. 241 (1974).

49. *See* Abbott B. Lipsky, Jr., *Reconciling* Red Lion *and* Tornillo: *A Consistent Theory of Media Regulation*, 28 STAN. L. REV. 563 (1978).

50. FORD ROWAN, BROADCAST FAIRNESS: DOCTRINE, PRACTICE, PROSPECTS 3 (1984) ("The FCC in the early 1980s moved to deregulate some aspects of broadcasting and urged Congress to abolish the Fairness Doctrine and the equal-time rule. . . . It should be noted how quickly the attitude had shifted toward deregulation . . .").

51. 47 U.S.C. § 230.

52. Niam Yaraghi, *Regulating Free Speech on Social Media Is Dangerous and Futile*, BROOKINGS (Sep. 21, 2018) ("Conservatives who support these policies argue that their freedom of speech is being undermined by social media companies who censor their voice.").

53. *Moody v. NetChoice, LLC; NetChoice, LLC v. Paxton*, 603 U.S. 707 (2024).

54. Melanie Hanson, *College Enrollment & Student Demographic Statistics*, EDUC. DATA INITIATIVE (Mar. 17, 2025).

55. Paul Horwitz, *Universities as First Amendment Institutions: Some Easy Answers and Hard Questions*, 54 UCLA L. REV. 1497, 1503–04 (2007) (arguing that courts should "recognize the unique social role played

by a variety of institutions," including universities and the press, whose "contribution to public discourse play a fundamental role in our system of free speech").

56. *Sweezy v. New Hampshire, by Wyman, Attorney General*, 354 U.S. 234, 242–43, 250, 261–63 (1957).

57. *Id.* at 263.

58. *Keyishian v. Bd. of Regents of Univ. of State of N.Y.*, 385 U.S. 589, 592, 603 (1967); Robert Post, *Assaulting Academic Freedom in the Age of Trump* 26 (Yale L. Sch. Pub. L. Rsch. Paper, 2025) (footnotes and internal citations omitted).

59. *Regents of Univ. of California v. Bakke*, 438 U.S. 265, 311–12 (1978).

60. *Id.* at 312–13.

61. *Students for Fair Admissions, Inc. v. President & Fellows of Harvard Coll.*, 600 U.S. 181 (2023); *see also Grutter v. Bollinger*, 539 U.S. 306 (2003).

CHAPTER THREE: THE FIFTH BRANCH

1. E. R. A. Seligman et al., *The 1915 Declaration of Principles: Academic Freedom and Tenure*, 40 BULL. AM. ASS'N UNIV. PROFESSORS 90, 98 (1954).

2. State Higher Education Executive Officers Association, *State Higher Education Finance (SHEF), Fiscal Year 2024* (2025) (figure 2.1, depicting a historical decline in the share of total funding coming from public sources as compared to tuition revenue); National Center for Science and Engineering Statistics, *Higher Education R&D Expenditures Increased 11.2%, Exceeded $108 Billion in FY 2023* (2024).

3. *See, e.g.*, Steven Levitsky, *The New Authoritarianism*, THE ATLANTIC (Feb. 10, 2025).

4. *See generally, e.g.*, WENDY BROWN, UNDOING THE DEMOS: NEOLIBERALISM'S STEALTH REVOLUTION (2015).

5. *See generally, e.g.*, THOMAS PIKETTY, CAPITAL IN THE 21ST CENTURY (2014); *See* Bureau of Labor Statistics, *Great Recession, Great Recovery? Trends from the Current Population Survey*, (Apr. 2018); *See* Gretchen Morgenson & Louise Story, *In Financial Crisis, No Prosecutions of Top Figures*, N.Y. TIMES (Apr. 14, 2011).

6. *See generally, e.g.,* STEVEN LEVITSKY & DANIEL ZIBLATT, TYRANNY OF THE MINORITY: WHY AMERICAN DEMOCRACY REACHED THE BREAKING POINT (2023); *Buckley v. Valeo,* 424 U.S. 1, 19–21 (1976) (equating money with speech for the first time by the Supreme Court).

7. *See* LEE BOLLINGER & GEOFFREY STONE, SOCIAL MEDIA, FREEDOM OF SPEECH, AND THE FUTURE OF OUR DEMOCRACY (2022).

8. *See* Kemal Kirişci et al., *Resistance to Erdoğan's Encroachment at Turkey's Top University, One Year On,* BROOKINGS INST. (Jan. 21, 2022); *see also* Benjamin Novak, *Pushed from Hungary, University Created by Soros Shifts to Vienna,* N.Y. TIMES (Nov. 15, 2019).

9. *See* JOHN STUART MILL, ON LIBERTY (1859).

10. *See, e.g.,* Exec. Order No. 14246, 90 Fed. Reg. 13997 (Mar. 28, 2025) ("Addressing Risks from Jenner & Block"); *see also* Exec. Order No. 14173, 90 Fed. Reg. 8633 (Jan. 25, 2025) ("Ending Illegal Discrimination and Restoring Merit-Based Opportunity").

11. *See, e.g.,* Jake Offenhartz, *Under Threat from Trump, Columbia University Agrees to Policy Changes,* AP NEWS (Mar. 21, 2025); *See* Alan Blinder, *Penn Agrees to Limit Participation of Transgender Athletes,* N.Y. TIMES (July 1, 2025).

12. *See* Max Eden, *A Comprehensive Guide to Overhauling Higher Education,* AMERICAN ENTERPRISE INSTITUTE (Dec. 4, 2024) ("the Justice Department should thoroughly explore indicting former Columbia President Lee Bollinger for fraud if he, through commission or omission, played a role in Columbia's submission of inaccurate data to *US News and World Report*").

13. Steff Danielle Thomas, *Paramount, Skydance Expected to Close Deal on Aug. 7,* THE HILL (July 26, 2025); *Alexander v. Trump,* 404 So. 3d 425 (Fla. Dist. Ct. App. 2025).

14. *See generally,* MARK TUSHNET, THE NAACP's LEGAL STRATEGY AGAINST SEGREGATED EDUCATION, 1925–1950 (1987); *See, e.g.,* Jedediah Purdy, *The Long Environmental Justice Movement,* 44 ECOLOGY LAW QUARTERLY 809 (2018); *see also* C. Edwin Baker, *The Independent Significance of the Press Clause under Existing Law,* 35 HOFSTRA L. REV. 955 (2007) (discussing discrete press rights and how they came to be recognized).

15. *See Branzburg*, 408 U.S. at 690–91.

16. *President & Fellows of Harvard College v. United States Department of Health & Human Services, et al.*, 25-cv-11048 (D. Mass. 2025); *American Association of University Professors—Harvard Faculty Chapter et al. v. United States Department of Justice, et al.*, 25-cv-10910 (D. Mass. 2025).

17. M.I. CONST. art. VIII, § 5 ("[e]ach board [of university trustees] shall have general supervision of its institution and the control and direction of all expenditures from the institution's funds"); *see also Regents of Univ. of Michigan v. State*, 235 N.W. 2d 1, 6 (1975) (interpreting this constitutional provision and noting that, while the state legislature may impose some conditions on appropriations, it "may not interfere with the management and control of those institutions [public universities]").

18. Bill Stall & Dan Morain, *Prop. 209 Wins, Bars Affirmative Action*, L.A. TIMES (Nov. 6, 1996); *see Grutter v. Bollinger*, 539 U.S. 306 (2003) (law school admissions case); *see also Gratz v. Bollinger*, 539 U.S. 244, 255 (2003) (undergraduate admissions case).

19. Gerald R. Ford, *Inclusive America, under Attack*, N.Y. TIMES (Aug. 8, 1999).

20. *See, e.g.,* Brief of Harvard University et al. as Amici Curiae in Support of Respondents, *Grutter*, 539 U.S. 306; *see also* Brief of the Association of American Colleges and Universities, et al. as Amici Curiae in Support of Respondents, *Id.*; *see also* Brief of 65 Leading American Businesses as Amici Curiae in Support of Respondents, *Id.; see also* Consolidated Brief of Lt. Gen. Julius W. Becton, Jr., et al. in Support of Respondents, *Id.*

21. Press Release, DOJ, HHS, ED, and GSA Announce Initial Cancelation of Grants and Contracts to Columbia University Worth $400 Million (July 22, 2025).

22. *See, e.g., Tinker,* 393 U.S. at 513 (noting that strong First Amendment protections with students must be coextensive with the ability for schools to manage conduct that disrupts classwork or involves substantial disorder or invasion of the rights of others).

23. *See* NEW YORKER, Cover (Oct. 8, 2007).

24. Manuel Roig-Franzia & Laura Wagner, *The Washington Post Says It Will Not Endorse a Candidate for President*, WASHINGTON POST (Oct. 25, 2024).

25. 438 U.S. 265, 307, 311–12 (1978) ("[t]he atmosphere of 'speculation, experiment and creation'—so essential to the quality of higher education—is widely believed to be promoted by a diverse student body") (citation omitted); *Grutter*, 539 U.S. 306; *SFFA*, 600 U.S. 181, 213–14 ("[a]lthough these are commendable goals [raised by Harvard and UNC], they are not sufficiently coherent for purposes of strict scrutiny").

26. University of Chicago, Kalven Committee, *Report on the University's Role in Political and Social Action*, 1 U. CHI. RECORD 1 (Nov. 11, 1967).

27. *See* 35 U.S.C. §§ 200–212 ("Bayh-Dole Act") (allowing universities to retain ownership of assets developed with federal research funding).

28. MONTAIGNE, *supra* Introduction note 8, at 815.